DEFENSE WILL NOT WIN
THE WAR

DEFENSE WILL NOT WIN THE WAR

BY W. F. KERNAN
Lieutenant Colonel, U. S. Army

BOSTON

LITTLE, BROWN AND COMPANY

1942

PRINTED IN THE UNITED STATES OF AMERICA

TO

ALICIA

PREFACE

THIS book represents the attempt of a professional soldier to orientate American public opinion in respect to offensive warfare. It has often been necessary for the author to diverge sharply from the judgments of our "military experts" and to point out fallacies in arguments which we had hitherto regarded as irrefutable. It has also been necessary to submit to a critical examination the war effort of the European democracies. However, this has been done in the firm belief that in order to defeat the Axis, we must learn every lesson which this war holds for us, even though such lessons emphasize the mistakes of our oracles and the strategic blunders of our allies.

The same thing goes for the victories of our enemies. It will not be sufficient for us to know that Hitler has conquered thus far because he possessed a superior army. We must learn why his army was superior. We must learn chapter and verse of his strategy and tactics in order that we may be under no illusions as regards the magnitude of the task that lies before us. We must learn, for example, that the general staffs of the European democracies suffered defeat mainly because they were thoroughly impregnated with "defense" ideas; that is to say, because they could not conceive of a German offensive which would abandon the time and space factors of 1918 and seek immediate victory by increasing the force factor far beyond the bounds of what the High Command regarded as reasonable. As late as 1939, even as late as 1941, the democracies had not grasped the essential elements of the Nazi war doctrine, i.e., that if mass represents space and force, mobility plus mass represents time and space and force. They had not grasped the fact that mobility and mass may be stepped up to a point beyond which no line will hold, no fortification stand and no merely defensive use of guns, tanks and planes will avail.

Now all these lessons are really lessons of history and to understand their meaning for America today, we must go beyond the First World War. Did the campaigns of Montenotte and Marengo teach the Austrians how to meet the Napoleonic attack? Isn't it true that Hohenlohe at Jena made the same mistakes that brought about the defeat of Mack at Ulm, that the Archduke Charles, for all of his experience at Ratisbon, simply could not learn the correct *riposte* to the deadly Napoleonic thrust? Why not? The answer is easy. These generals of the "old school" were thinking defensively. They elected to hold, to wait, to occupy, to disperse their forces. Napoleon elected to advance, to attack. His was the selection of time and place (*"La justesse des combinaisons"*), his the choice of means, of weapons to be used, of masses to be set in motion (*"Le Moyen"*) — his, in short, was the initiative and in that "total war" which we look back on across a century and a half, as in the total war of today, the initiative was everything.

But "the Bourbons never learn anything and never forget anything" and, in this respect, the generals of 1939, 1940, and 1941 — the Coraps, the Gorts, the Gamelins, the Shorts and the Kimmels — are no different from the "mules of Frederick the Great" who organized the defense of Europe in 1800. They did not see that in total warfare the initiative is always in the hands of the attacker. They never learned that to leave the initiative to the enemy in this sort of war is to leave to him infinite possibilities of attack and it is also to limit infinitely the means and methods of the defense.

That was what the "Austrian" school did in the Napoleonic Era and that was what the democratic "defense" school did in the sort of warfare which, let us hope, ended forever with the Japanese attack on Pearl Harbor. Nevertheless, we are still entitled to ask, how did it happen? Why was the same mistake repeated over and over again by two sets of generals with a century and a half in between the two sets of glaring military blunders? Again the answer is easy. In the first case, that of Napoleonic total warfare, it happened because of the influence of the small dynastic wars of the seventeenth and eighteenth centuries — wars which were, as Foch has pointed out, dominated by the principle of economy of the armed force ("*conservation de la force armée*"). In our own case, that of Nazi total war, the same thing happened because the military minds in control were under the influence of the limited "imperialistic" wars of

the nineteenth century whose dominating concept
was the supremacy of sea power.

Because America is the sole power left on earth
with sufficient strength to undertake an offensive,
we cannot afford to let these lessons go unheeded.
If we are not to pay an outrageous price for the
knowledge that against the offensive warfare of
today defense is not enough, the nations as well
as the army must understand the meaning of the
tragic events of the last two years. We must learn
not to confide too hopefully in any line that may
not be passed or any ocean that may not be crossed
by the enemy. We must learn and commit to
memory the truth that no single weapon or group
of weapons, no single fool-proof principle of
tactics or strategy, no fleet, is enough to defeat
Hitler as long as we continue to think defensively.
It is out of this sure and certain knowledge that
the victorious American offensive will spring. For
once the shackles of the defense myth are thrown
off, strategy becomes free to import the element
of surprise into operations, to do what the enemy
least expects; tactics will attack its objectives, not
with any stereotyped methods, but with an infinitude of combinations put into play by American

resourcefulness as the situation demands. To do this is to think offensively. But to think offensively, with the resources at our disposal, is to win the war.

The opinions expressed in the following pages are not in any sense of the word official. The facts have been taken from the ordinary historical sources and from carefully authenticated press reports. But for the importance attributed to these facts, as for the conclusions drawn therefrom, the author alone is responsible.

Fort Sill, Oklahoma.
January 19, 1942.

CONTENTS

DEFENSE WILL NOT WIN
THE WAR

CHAPTER I

THE DEFENSE MYTH

AMERICA has always been reluctant to read her horoscope in the skies of other continents. Faithful as we were to the dogma of our invulnerability, secure in the knowledge of our naval supremacy, the crescendo of sound and fury in the Eastern Hemisphere had aroused us to little more than a fidget of "defense measures" against a world indubitably mad, but comfortably beyond our borders. On the other side of our ocean ramparts, the heathen might rage and the regimental masses imagine a vain thing, but we, the children born to the democratic purple, were safe from attack under the beneficent gun turrets of our floating fortresses. It was our destiny, we told ourselves, to avoid all foreign entanglements by becoming the "arsenal of democracy" and with characteristic American ingenuity we invented a scheme for saving civilization, without risk, without danger and without the troublesome necessity of land warfare — all that was necessary was to put up a bold front, draw a line on a map and say: "Thus far and no farther."

With the Japanese attack on Pearl Harbor and the Axis declaration of war, the American dream changed like a kaleidoscope. We had thought that defense was enough to maintain our isolation and our entire military policy was oriented towards that end. We find ourselves committed to a conflict of civilizations, of cultures, of continents. We find, moreover, that the sort of warfare for which we have been preparing for the last twenty years is precisely the sort of warfare that led France to her doom and brought England to the edge of the abyss. For the problem that now confronts us, the question that must be answered is not, "How can we defend ourselves?" but "How can the war be taken to the enemy?" How can the striking power of the Axis be threatened at its source? When, and by what means, is democracy going to be enabled to launch its counterattack?

Thus at the very time when an American Expeditionary Force was the one thing we hoped would not be required of us, the relentless advance of the Axis forces upon us the adoption of an aggressive military technique. Hitler has overrun so many impassable frontiers, penetrated so many impregnable fortifications, enslaved so many defenders of democracy that our greatest, indeed our only real danger lies in permitting him to keep the initiative. From a soldier's standpoint the inference to be drawn is as simple as it is inescapable. If we are to retain the status of free men, we must mount an offensive. This is the one chance left to us. If we fail to take it, or if we delay too long, we shall find ourselves in due course of time standing meekly alongside of the Old Men of Vichy.

The first step towards a solution of our problem must be the rejection of all wishful thinking. We must return to reality — and to realism. Before the road to victory, and peace, can be traversed, it must be discovered. And by the same token all blind alleys and dead ends must be clearly marked. Our own weaknesses as well as those of our democratic allies must be subjected to a cold and impartial examination with the end in view of determining the mistakes that, whatever the cost, must not be committed again.

For it was not due wholly to the pre-eminent military genius of Hitler that the Axis achieved its present superiority. And it was not fortuitously or by chance that democracy was brought to the present necessity of fighting a world war for self-preservation. There was, as we are now beginning to suspect, something tragically, almost fatally wrong with our international outlook; some vicious fallacy, which we fondly believed to be self-evident truth, held us inert and complacent while our enemies were advancing with the sureness of tread and fixity of purpose of an Iroquois scalping party.

We remember now that before Pearl Harbor was bombed with malice aforethought the *Panay* was bombed "by accident," that the slaying of a British admiral on the bridge of *H.M.S. Prince of Wales* in the Singapore roadstead was preceded by the machine-gunning of a British ambassador on the road to Shanghai, and, as we read of the Japanese landing on the island of Luzon, in December 1941, we recalled how easy we made it for the Japanese to occupy the island of Hainan in December 1938, even going so far as to abandon our plans for the fortifications of Guam for fear of giving offense to what Senator Borah called a "friendly Pacific power." We watched the Japanese advance in Manchukuo and China, just as we watched the German advance in Europe, with the same sense of security and the same feeling of thankfulness that we were not, like other nations, subject to the vicissitudes of time and circumstance — and war. It is not that we were asleep, or mad, or unaware of what was going on about us. On the contrary, our perception of world affairs was never keener than during the critical years when the creeping-up and pegging-down activities of the Axis were at their peak. It is simply that we were in the grip of a false concept. Twenty-five years of peace and the endless repetition of certain shibboleths had given rise to a sort of collective delusion on the subject of armed combat between nations.

2

It has been said that "thinking is hard work, but prejudice is a pleasure," which is probably why reason is always at such a disadvantage when it finds itself in opposition to public opinion. The fate of Socrates is a case in point. One recalls also an incident in the *Iliad* where Laocoön was strangled by large serpents for telling his countrymen the unwelcome truth about the wooden horse. And in America during the past ten years anyone who brazenly advocated offensive strategy would have been promptly indicted as a "warmonger" — a word which our rampart watchers of press and pulpit never mentioned without crossing themselves against the Evil Eye.

If it is true that nations have the sort of government they deserve, it is also true that they have the sort of war they deserve. Where the sense of justice is asleep, where public opinion is no longer alert to detect the most distant menace to freedom, where fear of change deadens the body politic to the first flick of the whip of tyranny, a nation may be fairly said to have earned its yoke. Why should it be otherwise with war, which, however and for whatever causes it arises, is always the end term of the state — the *ultima ratio* or last argument of policy — expressing the supreme effort of a people to achieve its destiny? And just as government, as Washington pointed out, is "something more than influence," so war is more than a symposium of defense measures. An adequate military policy must be able to harden immediately into the spearhead of offensive warfare.

In the democracies of England, France and America, during what used to be called the "world crisis," war was a word which was on everyone's lips and yet it had lost practically all of its value as a reliable referent to objective reality. To be more exact, it was no longer the symbol of a *thing* or even the index of a *thought*, if by *thought* we mean a rational process: it was simply a sign which tripped an emotional reflex and which was used by the propagandists to give force and direction to the hatreds, fears and ambitions of men. Nobody stopped to think that war, even offensive war in the grand old manner, might have a proper and rational object, namely: the prevention of aggression; nobody called attention to the fact that war is an art which admits of the use of the intelligence, but differs from the other arts in that it cannot properly be exercised without risk. All of this muddle-headedness resulted in the "defense myth" which, with its corollaries, the absolute supremacy of sea power and the staff complex, furnished the groundwork for Hitler's sweeping military successes.

It should not be so very difficult for the American people, with its Yankee shrewdness, native mother-wit and hard common sense, to understand what it was that happened. Hitler, taking fullest advantage of the weakness of the democracies, particularly of their lack of decision in this matter of offensive warfare, has established and put into action a machine, a veritable juggernaut, which no mere defensive system, however strong, can hope to stop. Leave the initiative to him, let him select the time and method of attack and he will scale every rampart, take every fortress that mortal man can devise.

So carefully has he prepared this instrument, to such an extent has the German war machine perfected its technique of the offensive, that it can be counted upon to go on winning victories for him as long as his enemies and prospective victims obligingly go on taking the defensive against him. Before long it will not even be necessary for Hitler himself to man the controls. Anyone, Göring, Ribbentrop, Goebbels, with enough energy and intelligence to select an objective will be able to achieve the same results.

It was not without reason that the words *"Ich aber beschloss ein Politiker zu werden"* were carved on the base of Hitler's bust in Pasewalk. And if we of the democratic tradition are not careful, we shall wake up some fine morning and be able to decipher only too well the meaning of this fateful decision. What we must realize is that there is one aspect of Hitler's warfare which goes considerably beyond anything that has yet been devised for the conquest of other nations. I refer to that adroit and extensive use of propaganda which paralyzes public opinion prior to the military advance and is carefully calculated to achieve a single definite object — the prevention of an attack on the part of the selected victim.

For this neurotic Austrian who set forth in 1932 with the avowed purpose of enslaving a world understood two things very clearly. The guardians of freedom were the democracies. And in every democracy on earth, the paramount object of policy was avoidance of war. What then was Hitler's goal, upon his accession to power, except to induce in these countries whose governments

depended for their existence on the vote the notion that absolute offensive warfare need never be
waged? Victory without risk! Peace without sacrifice! All democracy had to do was to maintain its
defenses. The idea was so supremely delightful to
the free nations of the Christian West that even
now, with the hot breath of the Nazist assassins on
their necks, with the totalitarian dagger poised
over their very hearts, they have not been able to
abandon it.

3

"Ich aber beschloss ein Politiker zu werden."
What does this mean, translated in the light of recent events, but "I resolved to take advantage of
the power which ideas, even though they be false,
may obtain over the minds of men when they are
in accordance with the desires of men"? Now, in
the second quarter of the twentieth century, what
the men of the democratic tradition desired more
than anything else was peace, what they feared more
than anything else was war. And this desire and
this fear would be Hitler's master key to empire.

Building an instrument to take the fullest advantage of it, his army, committed always to the offensive, going to battle like a bridegroom to his bride, would move from strength to strength.

The waters through which he must pass would seem impassable, the sky would be overcast and at times his whole horizon would be black with ominous warning, but he had gotten hold of a truth and it would be a rock under his feet. The West, the Christian West, was afraid of war. In the so-called democracies whose doom had been predicted by his master in philosophy — Oswald Spengler — anything and everything would be endured, suffered and forgiven if only the tragic and passionate drama of armed combat might be avoided. Governments would maintain themselves in power by promises of peace, statesmen would be acclaimed for acts of cowardice committed in the name of security, armies would develop techniques that were calculated to guarantee them forever against the risks of fighting decisive battles, generals would be selected and endowed with the supreme command because of their avowed devotion to principles of defensive strategy which were the absolute negation of the art of war.

So Hitler developed on his part a system that worked like a slot machine and turned out a jackpot every time the lever was pulled. Were you a peace-loving commercial nation like Norway or Holland with nothing so far from your thoughts as that someday you might have to fight? Very good! You would hear on all sides the reassuring doctrine that your value to Germany was far greater as an autonomous neutral, that the cost of conquering you *vi et armis* would exceed the benefits to be derived from your friendly cooperation. Nothing would be allowed to disturb your peace of mind and no provocation would be offered you until the appropriate moment arrived for your assassination. Even then you would be graciously relieved from all necessity of combat. Your pet bugbear of war would never really confront you and the peace of slavery would be yours without the anguish of having to fight for freedom.

For the least, though as yet unheralded, stroke of Hitler's genius was this — that under his skillful hand, peace-loving nations passed painlessly from life to death (which is a sort of peace) without ever having to undergo the agony of war. That was the way it was with the neutral nations whom Hitler absorbed overnight without the necessity of swallowing twice. France was the next in line for the application of the soothing opiate of Nazi propaganda and, being an active belligerent, must be treated in a somewhat different fashion. France was in arms, had mobilized her reserves and possessed an army of several million said to be the finest in the world. In due course of time her destined destruction would be accomplished, but it was first necessary to employ the softening influence of the defense myth before the tanks and bombers could attack with that sense of the enemy's weakness without which Hitler never advances.

France, comfortably employed during the fall of 1939 in working the elevators and air-conditioning apparatus of her fortresses, must be persuaded (*a*) that her defense system was adequate and impregnable, (*b*) that Hitler, overawed by her military strength, was afraid to attack. In the initial stages of the war that began in September 1939, the world was treated to one of the most brilliant ruses of military history. Consider for a moment the *mis en scène:* the entire German strength was massed on the Polish border; the fortifications of the Limes Lines were far from complete; Hitler, for whom the hour of destiny had struck, had to utilize the striking power of his army to smash the Poles (if he were even temporarily halted in his advance to the east he was lost). Consequently, for two months at least his western flank was absolutely at the mercy of a French offensive. And here we recall inevitably the dictum of Foch, "A general with even the simplest knowledge of war would have ordered an attack." Had Gamelin done so the war would have been over in a month.

But there was never the remotest chance of the French launching an offensive as long as Hitler's propaganda was successful, i.e. as long as the French could be persuaded that defense was enough and that the war could be won without fighting. And it was to be that way up to the very end. The fallacies, the idea-myths would wage victorious warfare in the minds of Frenchmen who had long ago given up hard manliness for the sweet reasonableness of wishful thinking. It was so easy to believe that the British blockade was bound to be successful, that Russia would throw in with the allies and attack Hitler's rear at exactly the right moment. It was so easy to believe that the encirclement of Germany was complete and that all one had to do was to sit and wait until the tree-ripened fruit of victory fell into one's lap. "*Ma foi! But he is a stupid one — the Boche!*"

I say it was easy for Frenchmen to think these things because it was made easy for them by Adolf Hitler, because "facts" were created to drive home thoughts and thoughts hardened into convictions by the desire of an easy war and an effortless peace. In the initial stages of this sort of warfare, before the legions of Hannibal are unleashed, there is always a period of idea incubation when it is exceedingly difficult to distinguish between truth and fiction and the dominating factor is always the wish itself. Once it was clearly established that France did not desire to fight an active aggressive war, the rest was easy. From now on it would be no trouble whatsoever to get Frenchmen to swallow such facts as the continued attempts at fraternization made by Germans along the western front, the reluctance of German sea raiders to fire on French ships, the strange unwillingness of

German planes to drop bombs on French cities, the failure of Italy to declare war. All of these things seemed to add up to one conclusion: it would not be necessary for France to mount an offensive and the war could be won by sitting still in the fortifications of the Maginot Line. That was what every Frenchman wanted.

The war could be won without fighting and that was what happened in the end, only it was won by Germany rather than by France. For if a nation is really determined not to fight, ardently desires not to fight, and prefers to endure anything rather than risk a decisive campaign, something like this is practically bound to happen. From one point of view, Wellington was right when he said: "The only thing that is sadder than a great victory is a great defeat." But from another and entirely different point of view Gamelin was also right when he decided that if one can't win a war without fighting the next best thing is to lose it without fighting. From this latter viewpoint, if fighting means offensive combat, then there must be no fighting, and if offensive combat in the grand old manner means war, then there will be no war. A knife does not war with cheese, it cuts through it;

and an army does not war with the chaos and military incompetence that was France after the Sedan break-through. It thrusts it aside and passes on its way towards more important objectives.

CHAPTER II

THE STAFF COMPLEX

As FAR back as 1934 General Charles de Gaulle, foreseeing the inevitable conflict with Germany, had pointed out the futility of the French defense plan — even though that plan was based on the supposedly impregnable fortifications of the Maginot Line and the supposedly invincible sea power of the British fleet. General de Gaulle, moreover, had observed the German passion for planning carefully articulated offensives and had accurately calculated that, as against Teuton efficiency and attention to detail, no passive defense supported by blockade could possibly furnish a solution. In *The Army of the Future*, a treatise that was as charged with prophecy and as unheeded by the nation to whom it was addressed as the Book of Habakkuk, he had written: —

> The Teuton adversary, a methodical organizer, excels in delivering extremely violent

onslaughts from the outset. . . . The defenders, if they remain inactive, find themselves surprised, immobilized and outflanked. If, on the other hand, they are mobile and enterprising they take the initiative themselves. This is the only sensible attitude to adopt toward the German, who, unequaled in carrying out plans he has prepared, loses his grip as soon as he is attacked in a way he does not expect and shows an awkwardness in adapting himself to unforeseen circumstances.

To such an extent had the defense myth — that military hypertrophy of the pacifist twenties — gained a hold on the General Staffs of England and France that in 1934 de Gaulle was merely another voice crying in the wilderness. It is important to note, however, that forty years before Lieutenant Colonel Ferdinand Foch, Instructor at the *École Supérieure de la Guerre*, was preaching the same doctrine — a doctrine which as Marshal of France he was subsequently to employ for the discomfiture of that able plan maker, General von Ludendorff. In his book, *The Conduct of War*, published in 1892, Foch had emphasized two points that have assumed a startling significance in connection with de Gaulle's central thesis and the machinelike German advance now threatening the world. They may be summarized as follows: —

First: The German offensive strategy is wholly dependent on careful preparation made in accordance with a preconceived situation and resulting inevitably in a "battle of hypothesis," i.e. a battle in which the enemy, assumed to be on the defensive, is bound to be defeated as long as he does what is expected of him.

Second: The correct answer to the German battle of hypothesis is the "battle of maneuver" in which "the offensive, unleashed in all its glory, springs from the strategic concentration like lightning from a thunder cloud." To upset, throw out of axis (*"désaxer"*) the carefully prepared plan of the German strategist is to defeat him. For "the mules of Frederick have never become horses; after a century and a half of constant, unremitting effort, they still remain mules."

Does such a doctrine now seem bold to the point of rashness to military critics nurtured on the strategy of the concrete, for whom Hitler has already begun to be invested with the aura of invincibility? But Napoleon, the uncontested master

of the art of war, had said practically the same
thing: —

> The Austrian generals are good generals
> but they see too many things. As for me, I
> see only one thing — the enemy's masses.
> These I attack, secure in the knowledge that
> with their defeat everything else will fall into
> my hands.

And Napoleon also, who saw and commented
upon most of the difficulties of generalship, had
already flashed the torch of his genius on the
obstacle that was to prove insurmountable to the
Allied commanders in 1939: —

> What strength of will and greatness of soul
> it takes to launch one of those decisive battles
> on which the fate of a throne, a dynasty or a
> nation depends! — the necessary decision is too
> often lacking.

That, in fact, was precisely what happened on
May 10, 1940, when the German armies crossed the
borders of Belgium, Luxembourg and Holland.
The necessary decision was lacking. Neither
Gamelin nor Gort nor Corap could find the

necessary strength of will to say: "Here on the terrain selected by me, at the time determined by me, under conditions imposed upon the enemy by me, a battle will be fought which will decide the fate of Europe for the next thousand years." The result was that Hitler said it.

For twenty years the General Staffs of the democracies had held up to ridicule the strident "*Attaquez*" of Foch. For twenty years it had been taught in England and France that the defensive possesses a natural superiority over the offensive, that there is something inherently wrong about an all-out attack launched in the expectation of decisive victory because it runs the risk of decisive defeat. The British strategists who were thoroughly impregnated by the notion of "limited liability" and the supremacy of sea power, the French tacticians who had relegated the ideas of de Gaulle to the special limbo reserved by military conservatives for "visionary" conceptions, had all agreed that the ancient maxim of love and war, "*toujours l'audace*," was wrong. A kind of warfare resulted in which generals refused to take the initiative because they were unwilling to take the responsibility of ordering an attack. Therefore the initiative, the very mainspring of victory, was left to the enemy. The degradation of strategy, a high art in its own right, has never been more complete.

2

There is a point here that must be made as clear as noonday to every American citizen, whether he be soldier, sailor or taxpayer, because the safety of the Republic is involved in it. Let us note and remember that it is not mere weight of metal, or numbers, or volume of fire hurled against a carefully selected objective in accordance with a carefully drawn plan that constitutes the infallible recipe for victory. It is not sufficient merely to assemble an appropriate mass of tanks, bombers, artillery and infantry and send them against the enemy's flank or center in order to win a battle of the first class. In other words strategy is something more than the application of force and even tactics is more than applied mechanics. It is true that the Germans think so and have continued to think so since the days of Frederick the Great and it is true, too, that Hitler has been thus far successful due to his unswerving devotion to this concept. Nevertheless, as Foch pointed out, "the whole art of war does not consist in rushing upon the enemy like a mad bull."

Nor, we might add, does it consist in building a line of trenches, or of concrete and steel emplacements, and deciding to hold at all costs. In the defense as in the attack, the three strategic variables, time, space and force, must still be correctly combined. It is easy for a general to say, "They shall not pass," as Pétain said at Verdun, or to call on every soldier to "die in his tracks rather than yield an inch," as Weygand said at Sedan. But in such cases all initiative is left in the hands of the enemy, and the art of command becomes little more than a matter of transporting ammunition and ordering in the reserves. Whether the line holds, as it held at Verdun, or breaks as it broke at Sedan depends on the native qualities of a race, on that indefinable imponderable of war called "morale." But whether won or lost, the so-called "soldiers' battle" with its useless slaughter constitutes the gravest indictment that can be brought against generalship.

The Staff Complex

And it was precisely here that the generalship of the European democracies failed in 1940 and 1941 under the hammer blows of Hitler's *Panzer* divisions. Due to an excessive concentration on purely staff functions, there had been in France and England a tendency to submerge the commander in the work of his staff. So far had this been carried in the decade before the Sedan break-through that when the four "G's" [1] had finished "processing" an operation in all its voluminous detail no general born of woman, not even if he possessed the combined military abilities of Hannibal, Julius Caesar and Stonewall Jackson, could have put the resulting plan into execution without undue dependence on some subordinate.

I say "undue" dependence, for no one will deny that any commander worthy of the name must always be to a very great extent dependent on his staff. But there is one burden that he must always bear on his own shoulders and that is the responsibility of making a decision. Now it is in the initial decision ("How shall the attack be

[1] G1, Personnel; G2, Intelligence; G3, War Plans and Training; G4, Supply.

27

launched?") and again in the selection of the time and method of the counterattack that the art of generalship consists. And it is in this respect that French and British strategy have completely failed in the present war.

The most carefully prepared plans, made by the most efficient staff, do not furnish a solution to the problem presented by an aggressive and highly mobile enemy. What is needed is a decision that envisages the essential elements of the situation. But mired down in plans that no longer correspond to the realities, blinded and hampered by the rush of events, which the staff for lack of time are unable to correlate, the Allied High Command abdicates. The armies of Gamelin and Gort are herded like sheep.

The nerve of the whole matter of command is contained in the following remark of Napoleon, long held to be mysterious, but now clear as noonday in the light of the volcanic events of the past year: —

> Plan of operations! I never had a plan of operations. I advance in the center of my *bataillon carré* secure in the knowledge that

wherever I encounter the enemy my superior power of maneuver will enable me to defeat him.

The whole secret of the art of the commander which is the whole secret of the art of war is in this sentence with its hidden precept that can never be carried out by any staff officer however capable. For after all the formulae for organization and tactical dispositions have been complied with, after the ammunition has been issued and the march table distributed, victory is still the fruit of a maneuver carried out *during the course of a battle* — a maneuver that cannot possibly be envisaged until the enemy is encountered and hence cannot possibly be the result of a plan prepared in advance. If, as Foch says, "the key to victory hangs in the tent of the commander," it is because only the commander is capable of meeting with a pregnant decision every development of a situation that, after contact is gained, is bound to suffer radical change.

But the French and British generals had not, alas! been trained in this school. With their elaborate plans for defense of the Maginot Line, Big and

Little; defense of the Meuse, defense of the Al-
bert Canal, defense of the Scheldt, even the fatal
advance of General Gort's British Army into
Belgium was simply a movement to occupy and
hold a line. When the defenses did not hold and
the line broke in half a dozen places at once, the
Allied commanders were helpless as babes to stem
the German advance. We all know how General
Georges, vainly endeavoring to make a last-min-
ute, last-ditch stand against the tanks of von Kleist,
was captured at Rethel on May 18, 1940 — he was
looking for his staff!

And by the same token, it is childish to seek
the reasons for Dunkirk and Sedan in the mistakes
of English ministers or the bickering of French
politicians. These defeats were military, not political or economic. Lee had far worse conditions to
combat in the Congress of the Confederacy than
anything Gamelin or Gort or Weygand ever
dreamed of, and yet he managed to win several
battles. Hannibal was forced to maintain himself in
Italy for twelve years without any support whatever from the Carthaginian Senate and yet Cannae
fails to show any evidence of the rifts in the home
front. What if British parliamentarians were given

to digressions concerning the text of Walton's *Compleat Angler* when they should have been discussing means of increasing the output of munitions! What if the enmity between the mistresses of Daladier and Reynaud caused these two estimable gentlemen grave annoyance! These little anecdotes are most interesting particularly when they come to us dressed in the colorful prose of M. André Maurois, but it is still well worth our while to discover the military reasons which operated to bring about the military debacle of 1940. How was it that with such a long start, with such vast sums spent on fortifications, with so much time for study and training, with so many resources at their disposal, the best generals of France and England were defeated in a single week?

I have said that these men were all ardent believers in the credo of the Maginot Line and that they had all accepted with the fervor of a religious dogma Mahan's theory of the absolute supremacy of British sea power. However it is not so much in these notions, false as they were, that we must seek the causes of the debacle. For us the real significance lies in the type of man, more particularly in the type of mind, that could spend twenty years building up a military system that would crack under the first blow of the enemy. If nations can be so easily destroyed in modern warfare, it is high time we learned something about it.

André Giraud has told us how after war was declared in 1939 Gamelin and his galaxy of staff officers sat comfortably ensconced at Vincennes discussing history and art while Hitler perfected his plans for the passage of the Meuse. We know also what the British Army was doing on its Belgian Front while Skoda was turning out the tanks that would give such a good account of themselves on the road to Dunkirk. The U.S.O. had not yet been conceived but various other movements to keep up morale were in full swing: "Art for the Armies," "Burlesque for the Armies," "Plays for the Armies" — everything in short was being thought of except "War for the Armies." Hitler, however, was making the necessary arrangements for that to be taken care of.

Long before the blow fell in May 1940, the peoples of France and England, with an instinctive feeling of impending danger, called on the High Command for some positive action against the implacable enemy who was massing his forces for the

Sedan break-through. They were told: "Whoever is the first to leave his shell in this war is going to be badly hurt." To young Frenchmen burning to measure swords with Hitler's famous shock troops, eager to mount one of those offensives which have saved France from her invaders time out of mind, Gamelin quoted complacently the dogma of the French General Staff, "The attack must have three times as many infantry effectives, six times as much artillery, twelve times as much ammunition if it hopes to overcome the defense." When Reynaud sent Gamelin a copy of de Gaulle's book, *The Army of the Future*, which made it plain as a pikestaff that mechanized forces and air power had radically changed the holding power of fortifications, the latter replied with a note saying magisterially, "It has interested me greatly, but I am not in agreement with your views."

No oriental potentate can be more mystical, more august, more unapproachable than your born-to-the-purple staff officer of the old "defense" school and, in the fall of 1939, practically every staff officer in the world outside Germany belonged to this school. In that Seventh Heaven of Brass Hats, guarded by the twin dragons of preconception and anonymity, rude reality must walk on tiptoe and every strident voice that would tell of time and circumstance must be hushed to a whisper. This is the Staff! Let no one, not even the enemy, dare to disturb the meditations of these military yogis who are busy manufacturing plans for some divine far-off event. And the mentality that goes with it is the staff complex, the mentality that merely by taking thought would make victory as certain as tomorrow's sunrise, the mentality that regards the incurring of risks in battle as slightly worse than treason and which refuses to advance until all danger is removed.

3

As a matter of fact, the staff system which was in force in the French and British Armies before the Sedan break-through was the exact military counterpart of the prevailing governmental system of those unfortunate countries during the period 1920–1940 — the years which in very truth the locust hath eaten. The statesmen like Clemenceau who believed it possible to cut the design for Utopia from the skin of the Boche; the diplomats like Simon who thought that peace without justice was desirable; the proconsuls, like Anthony Eden, who were convinced that the old balance of power would still work; the Chamberlains, Lavals, Daladiers who sought to maintain the status quo by undermining every real bulwark of European democracy — could such men control the policy of the two most powerful empires on earth for twenty years without having some influence on the generals who commanded their armies?

It is not enough to say that the enforced inertia of twenty years of peace is bound to have its effect on the army of a democracy, that without the constant menace of an active and hostile neighbor, any military system, no matter how vigorous and watchful it was originally, is bound to deteriorate. The truth is rather that the inherent weaknesses of a democracy are bound sooner or later to show up in the army and in the initial operations against the enemy. There are few — if any — of our military critics who realize the significance of the Japanese "surprise" attack on Pearl Harbor.

Now I do not deny the efficiency of the German High Command in devising a tactical instrument of tremendous striking power, but I still think it possible to demonstrate beyond a reasonable doubt that Hitler's enslavement of Europe in a single year was due not to any invincible military system, but to the weaknesses of the opposing armies — military weaknesses, which over a long period of time, from 1919 to 1939 to be exact, had so germinated and sprouted that in 1940 the field was ripe for harvest. Hitler's success has been due to plans that were carried out. The failure of the Allies in every operation from Narvik to the present campaign in Africa has been due to plans that by their very nature could not have been carried out.

In the face of confirmed reports concerning Hitler's troop concentrations and intentions on May 10, 1940, French and British generals were not only unwilling to attack, they were even reluctant to order the reserves forward for the strengthening of their lines. Up to the last fatal moment, when it was too late for any action to save the situation, they were hoping against hope that it would not be necessary to take any action.

How else can we explain Corap's failure to attack on the evening of May 9 when the German breakthrough had placed Guderian in a dangerous pocket where for at least six hours he risked annihilation if the French Commander had ordered an offensive. Here was certainly a situation where, as Foch said of the Prussian dispositions before Gravellotte, "A general with the simplest knowledge of war would have been able to upset the most careful plans by a resolute advance." But the staff mentality does not function in the realm of the real.

Chauvineau's book *Is Invasion Possible?* was accepted as gospel by the French General Staff and Chauvineau had taught that an attack, any attack, requires a vast superiority in effectives. The stereotyped hypothesis was that reserves were necessary; the reserves could not arrive before noon on the tenth, so the French attack to reduce the German salient and throw Guderian back across the Meuse was scheduled to take place the next morning. Did anyone remember, on that fatal day, the conversation that had taken place between Napoleon and Berthier when the former had ordered an attack on the Austrians at Ratisbon: —

37

BERTHIER: "Where are your reserves, Sire?"

NAPOLEON: "Reserves! Do you think I am Moreau?"

How else can one explain Gort's failure to mount an offensive when he finally reached the northern frontier of Belgium after moving his troops out of the Little Maginot Line and with the fullest possible information of the German concentrations opposite the Sedan "hinge"? Did anyone ever hear of an army being pulled out of fortified positions in order to defend an unfortified line? And yet that was exactly what the British Expeditionary Force was attempting to do. And if we ask why, the answer is simply that another theory was being entertained by the staff, which, although it was known to be in opposition to the reality, was still accepted and acted upon *because* the decisions and actions required by it had already been prepared in advance. It was assumed that the Ardennes Forest could be adequately defended by the Belgian Cavalry and that the main German thrust was coming from the north. Once more hypothesis had taken the place of reality.

At any rate there is a close parallel between the

conduct of military operations in the spring of 1940 and the conduct of diplomatic operations in the summer of 1939. In both cases, due to a false estimate of the situation and the false sense of security engendered thereby, decisions were made which were supposedly in accordance with the "facts" but which turned out to be in complete opposition to reality.

This paradox of an inherent conflict between the fact and the reality is to be observed in the entire conduct of the war thus far. It is a unique by-product of the staff complex and its familiar devil the defense myth. Of all the egregious errors that have plagued the world since the vanishing of the old *lex regia* and the concept that "the king can do no wrong," this notion of an international status quo that was unassailable and indestructible in its own right was surely the most tragic in its consequences.

Such was the strength of fortifications (as determined by the careful calculations and irrefutable figures of the staff), such was the strategic value of the territory in the hands of friendly powers (as estimated by the staff), such was the influence of sea power, of entrenched weapons, of economic reprisals (had not the staff figured that seventy-five per cent of the world's wealth was in the hands of the "well-disposed" nations?) that by no stretch of the imagination could any attack scale the towering ramparts of the three democracies. So it was accepted as a foregone conclusion that the carefully built, carefully guarded structure could not possibly fall for many generations to come. We fortunate ones born within the charmed circle of the impregnable outposts (Manila, Singapore, Malta, Dakar, Scapa Flow, Gibraltar) need never fear — "Peace for our time" was guaranteed to us.

CHAPTER III

MAHAN WAS WRONG!

IT IS time that the pedigree of this succubus that has fastened itself upon the art of war in the Western democracies should be clearly established. And with our hour of destiny upon us, it is time for us to realize that what our publicists and wishful thinkers have held to be the classic British strategy, with its adjunct of sea power, was never employed with success by the British or any other robust people in the face of a formidable enemy. The verdict of history is against it.

A good many of us seem to have forgotten that England owes her greatness and the British Empire its origin to a strategy that was offensive rather than defensive — to a generalship which, not content with erecting bastions or watching ramparts, was determined to carry fire and sword to the strongholds of the enemy. In the seventeenth and eighteenth centuries this did not mean only sea power, or mainly sea power. It meant the successful operation of armies on foreign soil. It produced the "Scarlet Caterpillar" of Marlborough that shamelessly invaded the territories of Louis XIV. It flowered quite naturally into decisive battles like Blenheim and Vitoria — and Waterloo.

For two hundred years Britain was engaged in a life-and-death struggle with continental dictators who bore more than a surface resemblance to our own Wild Man of Europe, and in every case the correct antidote was found in offensive warfare. That pugnacious liberalism that had humbled the proud Bourbon and put a spoke in the chariot wheel of the Corsican had no "defense doctrine" and no Maginot Line but it had a ferocious hatred of militarism. And it would fight at the drop of a hat, on provocation, on very weak provocation, sometimes on no provocation at all, whenever it detected a threat of universal aggression. It is certainly true that not since the dynastic feudal wars of the Middle Ages has England had any interest in the conquest of the nations of the continent and that there has been no attempt to extend British sovereignty to any portion of European soil. Nevertheless, time after time, England had a vital interest in preventing certain dictators from achieving the conquest of Europe and extending the sovereignty of a particular state over the other states of the European comity.

Now it was precisely this duality of aim, that is to say, self-limitation as regards the extension of British sovereignty over the other peoples of Europe — all-out, offensive war effort to prevent the domination of the continent by ambitious autocrats — that made England great. We Americans recognize this today and that is one reason why we are enlisted on the side of England in the present conflict. It is part of our own greatness that as a nation we were never wholly indifferent to that great principle for which England was fighting. But the shadow of the Swastika is lengthening, we ourselves are now in it up to the hilt and we cannot afford to make the same mistakes that England made.

Therefore it is important for us to understand that there came a time in the nineteenth century when England departed from her historic policy and when her historic strategy was modified to suit a brummagem imperialism. An Acton would warn that "Prussian militarism is the deadliest enemy the Anglo-Saxon race has ever encountered," and his warning would go unheeded. A Palmerston would advise that "England has no eternal enmities and no eternal friendships, she has only eternal interests," and his dictum would be hailed with acclamation. The old "balance of power" concept of Pitt and Burke that had been the guardian angel of British diplomacy would be streamlined by an abstraction called "imperial interest." From now on policy would be dominated by financial considerations, principles would be subordinated to expediency, and the signposts of the strategy of limited liability would point the road to Munich — and to Dunkirk.

It was during this period that the doctrinal godfather of the defense myth was born. The Mahan theory of a purely naval supremacy would have been laughed to scorn by the Englishmen of previous generations. It was received with adulation by the nineteenth-century imperialists. Here was the very concept the statesman of "Manchester" School needed: security without too much responsibility, prestige without the awful risks of land warfare. Here was a strategy that could never go wrong, that would make England the undisputed mistress of world commerce, the uncontested arbiter of the affairs of the "lesser nationalities," on the sole condition that a small percentage of the profits of "British Empire Ltd." be invested in ships of the line.

2

If Admiral Alfred Thayer Mahan had been right, Britain's Balkan adventure would not have ended in the spring of 1941 by a British Prime Minister exchanging congratulations with the Commons over the fact that forty thousand English and Australian troops had been re-embarked successfully off the shores of Greece. If Mahan had been right, the German Army would be caged in Central Europe and Britain would even now be selecting the strategic point for the final *coup de grace*. But alas! as Britain is beginning to find out, as America (unless she awakens in time) will discover, Mahan was wrong.

The "influence of sea power upon history" meant simply one thing: the supremacy of the

British Navy in the hundred years after Waterloo when the wars of Europe, owing to the general
exhaustion caused by Napoleon, were little more
than glorified cat fights. It was a noble theory for
the Victorian Age and destined to go far, a godsend for the armchair strategists who could babble
henceforth of "warm-water ports" and naval bases
without the remotest possibility of being contra-
dicted. Oh, it was a fine theory, magnificently
tricked out in the tinsel of false assumptions,
worthy of the bourgeois "defensive strategy"
which developed alongside it!

At its high point it would see a victorious peace
treaty signed in a railway car which the world
would hail as the end of the war to end war and
the unmistakable sign that the good old order would
endure forever. Afterward it would see a German
fleet scuttled at Scapa Flow and everybody would
say that the last possibility of the last threat to the
freedom of the seas was gone and would never
return. But a realist named Hitler was waiting for
this gallant theory round a bend in the road that
even as late as September 1939 seemed so distant
that it was hardly worth bothering about.

Mahan was wrong! And such was the influence

of his theory that even now, with the conquest of Europe accomplished in a year, a great many people find it difficult to understand what has happened to Western Civilization. From the Battle of Waterloo to the cracking of that bloated and pompous silliness called the Maginot Line, the grand strategy of the West had gone to sleep in the shadow cast by the myth of sea power. War was no longer "absolute" in the Napoleonic sense, and with the single exception of the superb military system of Foch, the fruits of whose victories were lost almost as soon as they were gained, the wars of Europe from 1815 to 1940 were like the games of children.

Fought under the paternal influence of British sea power, according to the rules laid down by British policy, such wars lacked the essential element of warfare — the risk of absolute, annihilating defeat. Whatever the outcome of a war like that fought by France and Prussia in 1870, it would not change the established order in Europe. No matter who won, the will of the victor would still be limited. Generals might make as many mistakes as they pleased, but the essential elements of the status quo would not be seriously changed. The

British fleet was always there to redress the military balance whenever it leaned too far to one side, just as British imperial policy was always there to redress the diplomatic balance whenever some incident at Fashoda, or elsewhere, set the sabers to rattling too loudly.

The great mistake, the well-nigh fatal error, lay in assuming that the cozy, tight little diplomacy of the post-Waterloo era would last forever. It was upon this assumption that Admiral Mahan had written his monumental treatise. And it was also upon this assumption that the "business as usual" slogan was still honored in Britain even after the declaration of war against Hitler in 1939. Now from 1815 to 1940 is a span of a century and a quarter, and that is a long time for any strategy — even the strategy of Britain's Victorian "cavalcade" — to refuse to face reality. And during this entire period it was believed in England (as it is believed in some influential quarters in America ·today) that sea power was sufficient to uphold Western Civilization to the end of time, that any threat launched against democracy could be parried, first, by the right combination of naval powers; second, by defending until the enemy wore

48

himself out in the attack. That is the way it has been for the past hundred and twenty-five years and that is why a surprisingly large number of people still talk and act as though the offensive land operations of armies were second in importance to sea power.

What these people fail to see is that we are no longer fighting dynastic, or territorial, or even national war. If defense was not enough to prevent the Catholic dynasts of the sixteenth century from bringing contemporary Protestant dynasts under the heel of religious intolerance; if defense was not enough to put a crimp in the desire of His Most Christian Majesty Louis XIV to cast his royal shoe over a British monarch who styled himself *Defensor Fidei*; if defense was not enough to stop Napoleon from dragging the canopy of his conquests and concordats over all Europe — by how much less will it suffice to rid the world of a pagan totalitarian coalition that is self-admittedly the enemy of everything our Christian civilization stands for?

The strange thing is that we obstinately refuse to recognize this. Strategically we are still living in the world of nineteenth-century "limited war."

Historically our minds are still functioning in a frame of reference whose co-ordinates are British imperialism and British sea power. It is war made in the shadow of a fleet so powerful that the generals are bound to come right side up every time no matter how many mistakes they make.

3

Mahan and the exponents of the sea power and empire concept did not know and, in the nature of things, could not have known of the tremendous influence the airplane was destined to wield over naval warfare in the second quarter of the twentieth century. Nevertheless, it is not by the theory of air power alone that one disproves the Mahan thesis. The argument is not that of capital ship versus bombing plane, and in this respect, the air experts who would seek to invest the nation's wealth in flying fortresses are just as muddle-headed as those who would solve the problem of how to beat the Axis by building another fleet of superdreadnaughts.

Mahan Was Wrong!

The truth is that Mahan's theory, like the theory of his air-power successors, was an oversimplification. In the world of the nineteenth century, with every nation of Europe (except England) impoverished by the Napoleonic wars and every nation (including England) apparently going all out for that particular brand of humanitarianism called world peace, it seemed reasonable to suppose that the supremacy enjoyed by Great Britain on the seas would persist to the end of time. All the world really needed was a police power and for this purpose the British fleet was ample. According to this theory, if you could get an economic foothold in an undeveloped country such as India, you could use your fleet to expand that foothold into complete political domination and what started as a British East India Company would end quite naturally in a British King proclaiming himself Emperor of India. In the same way, you could perch on the edge of a continent such as Africa and control that continent absolutely through the control of the seas surrounding it and in general you could establish bases all over the world and go around saying "The sun never sets on the British flag," and no one could offer any argument as long as the British fleet was there. In other words, you could come pretty near achieving economic control of the world in an epoch when economic control was the thing that counted, as long as your fleet was supreme.

Moreover, as long as your fleet was supreme, you could talk turkey to the chancelleries of your fellow European powers and have a pretty dog-gone good chance of being listened to because you had an instrument (the sea blockade) which was absolutely unanswerable as long as it could be applied successfully. It worked fine, so fine that even hard-boiled Americans like the elder Roosevelt began to imitate it, but the only reason why it worked was because it was never seriously challenged anywhere by a real continental bid for supremacy. Napoleon had tried to challenge it and might have been successful if he could have brought Russia to heel. The Kaiser tried to challenge it but was foolish enough to antagonize America at the wrong time and failed to get his hands on any real pay-dirt territory before he was bowled over by the weight of American man power and industry.

What I am saying is that neither Napoleon I nor Wilhelm II was ever able to establish a real continental system that would stand up against the British idea of an empire supported by sea power. Coming almost exactly a century apart, what the two threats did was this: The one weakened the old dynastic order in Europe and threw the fruits of industrial revolution into the lap of England; the other weakened the industrial civilization that had arisen in the shadow of British sea power and made possible the continental system of Hitler, Mussolini, Hirohito, *et alii.*

It should be evident by this time that Hitler succeeded where the other two challengers failed, because he was able to combine the essential Prussian idea of the dominating German race with the essentially Napoleonic idea of a United States of Europe. In the present epoch the Nazi with his shibboleths of economic security for all subject peoples of Hitler's world island has replaced the Frenchman of the Peace of Tilsit with his watchwords *Liberté, Égalité, Fraternité* for a Europe under the leadership of Napoleon.

The one offered freedom from the slavery imposed by the political royalists of the eighteenth century, the other offers freedom from the slavery imposed by the economic royalists of the nineteenth century. The one failed because to the sea power of Nelson was added the offensive land power of Wellington. The other has succeeded thus far because the sea-power theory has been carried to a logical conclusion by Britain and America and that conclusion has turned out to be a *reductio ad absurdum*. But neither the one nor the other had the slightest value unless it was supported by victorious generalship. The lesson we must learn from history is that in an all-out continental war (and this war is the daddy of them all) every effort that is not aimed at the heart of the enemy, that is to say at his central military force, is bound to be indecisive.

Since Germany was the first to waken from the dogmatic slumber of the Mahan theory; since Hitler suddenly conceived the notion that Napoleon's epigram "The whole British Navy is not worth one French bayonet" is not the arrant nonsense it has been generally supposed to be; since the German Army purge of 1937 ruthlessly weeded out the officers of the Administrative School of War and replaced them by commanders with some sense of the objective (a change that was regarded with horror by the Brass Hats of England, France and

54

America); since the armament and training and matériel of the German Army were carefully planned
with the idea in mind that sometime, somewhere,
somehow that army would attack, it is not, after
all, so very strange that the Axis spearheads have
had little difficulty in piercing the loins of nations
trained only in *defense*. Keeping these things in
mind, we shall be ready to take the next step
towards realism — and victory. The methods and
plans of the enemy must now be subjected to the
same cold and impartial analysis which disclosed
to us our own weaknesses.

CHAPTER IV

CONTINENTAL WARFARE AND GEOPOLITICS

FREDERICK THE GREAT had a stereotyped battle plan known as the "oblique order" which made him the dominant figure of Europe in the eighteenth century. It was designed to defeat French and Austrian generals who were still under the influence of medieval tactics and insisted on handling armies in the field as though they were castles to be defended. So Prussian infantrymen were trained to advance in line, shoulder to shoulder, holding their fire (and disregarding casualties) until they were within point-blank range. And since the enemy obligingly remained drawn up in dense squares and rectangles which presented excellent targets, Frederick won so often that the oblique order came to be regarded as a sort of standard recipe for victory by future generations of war-loving Germans.

Now this oblique order was a purely tactical formation which depended for its success on the rigidity of a moving line advancing always to the attack in accordance with a preconceived idea that the enemy would take up a position and attempt to hold it. One would have thought that Jena, where the "mules of Frederick" were pretty thoroughly flattened by Napoleon, would have put an end to it once and for all. But the Prussian is nothing if not obstinate. In the oblique order he had found a military conception which was peculiarly adapted to his genius for meticulous planning, and he was loath to depart from it. As a matter of fact he never did depart from it.

Moltke the Elder, octogenarian, archetype of all staff officers, was a disciple of Clausewitz and a firm believer in mass attack. He also wanted something that would enable his armies to advance like clockwork and win battles without the troublesome necessity of strategic reconnaissance. Result: the famous plan of 1870, which took over all the rigidity of Frederick's tactics and incorporated it into strategy. What had been a line of men now became a line of masses (divisions, corps, armies) which

57

advanced as relentlessly as the old Prussian grena-
diers on the assumption that the enemy was going
to do exactly what was expected of him.

The strategy of Moltke with its eighteenth-cen-
tury inheritance was completely successful, though,
as I have already pointed out, nobody stopped to
think what would have happened to this warfare
by hypothesis had the French been so inconsiderate
as to throw a wrench in the clockwork by an un-
suspected attack. Then came the von Schlieffen
Plan of 1914 with its identical conceptions — identical, I mean, with those of both Frederick and
Moltke, though providing for vastly extended lines
but still rigid, still wholly dependent on the con-
formance of reality with the original hypothesis.
And there are military critics who have already
seen a certain similarity between the German plans
of 1914 and 1940 and who are beginning to point
out that Hitler's blueprint for the enslavement of
Europe is nothing but the old von Schlieffen Plan
on a much more grandiose scale.

This is true as far as it goes, but what I am trying
to show is that it is a long way from being the
whole truth. It is not merely that Hitler has incorporated the von Schlieffen concept into his

strategy or even that he has carried out more thoroughly than his predecessor by means of tanks and aircraft the admonition to "make the right wing strong." For us, the really important thing is that Hitler has done exactly what he might have been expected to do, exactly what every war-minded German has done since the Battle of Rossbach in 1757. He has taken over the whole oblique order of Frederick and is applying it to the conquest of the world. Nations, peoples, continents and the islands of the sea are being encircled, besieged and absorbed — as though they were so many castles.

2

It is impossible to understand fully the meaning of the "continental warfare" now being waged by Nazi Germany without some reference to the doctrine of Haushofer and the geopoliticians. In its essence and stripped of the usual Teutonic verbiage, this doctrine is simply an all-out, thoroughgoing theoretical development of Hitler's original determination to exploit the dependence upon sea power that has long been manifest in British and American policy. It all boils down to this: you have one nation supreme upon the sea and with a very small military potential (England) and you have another nation (America) powerful upon the sea and with an enormous military potential but so far removed in space as to be *for the time being* negligible as a formidable land opponent. And both of these nations though utterly opposed to Germany and desiring nothing more than her destruction are still so devoted to the ancient nineteenth-century notion (the Mahan theory) of the supremacy of sea power that they are apparently unwilling to commit themselves, *for the time being* at any rate, to a major land offensive. The most that these nations have done thus far and, by all accounts, the most that they will do for some time to come will lie in the direction of the stepping-up of their vaunted sea power together with an increase in the air arm which, as conceived and used by them, is merely an extension of sea power into the third dimension.

Now with this devotion to sea power and air power to the exclusion of land power so manifest on the part of the democracies, it would be suicidal madness on the part of a warrior nation (Germany) whose ultimate objective is world supremacy not to take the fullest advantage of the opportunity thus presented. Neither sea power nor air power can take and hold terrain and it is on terrain, on this mother earth of ours and not on the sea or in the air, that man, the *genus homo* of this planet, lives. Therefore a plan for world domination must be evolved that will be squarely based on the taking and holding of terrain, an instrument will be created to carry out the plan, a strategy will be devised for the prompt and efficient employment of the instrument. The plan will be called geopolitics, the instrument will be the German Army, the strategy will be the continental warfare of Adolf Hitler and the whole business will be over, a *fait accompli* — like the annexation of Austria and the seizure of Czecho-Slovakia — before the ocean-bound democracies know what it is all about.

The Nazi Geopolitik has been made unnecessarily complicated by some of our publicists who find mysterious even such a lucid book as *Mein Kampf* but it is in reality very simple. If you happen to have a congeries of continents such as Europe, Asia and Africa, which lie within striking distance and occupation range of your armies, you will call it a "world island" and of the vast area thus defined (i.e. lands that can be reached without absolute sea supremacy) you will arbitrarily circumscribe a certain part and call it the "Heart Land."

You are now ready for the practice of geopolitics, for the core of the Heart Land — the heart within the heart of the World Island — is Germany, the warrior nation. And just as the human heart is not the abode or resting place of the blood which it tirelessly dispatches to the extremities of the human body, so the German people in the geopolitical concept are not to be regarded as indwellers or occupiers of the German homeland but rather as a sort of vital force or source of energy that sends the warrior race ever outwards and onwards until the entire area (*Lebensraum*) of the World Island, considered to be as much the birthright of the German nation as the body is the birthright of the blood, shall be completely occupied, i.e. subjugated.

There are, of course, as many different forms of this theory as there are geopoliticians among the Axis powers (Japan and Italy have also taken to it like sick chickens to a hot brick) but its cardinal principle, which, thus far, has been almost com-

pletely successful in its practical application, is that
Germany shall continue to attack until she is supreme in the carefully chosen field of action of her
armies and that her enemies, trusting to the efficacy
of sea power for the ultimate victory, shall continue
to defend and to furnish aid to all defenders of the
World Island wherever they may be.

With regard to the position of America in this
scheme there are several points that merit careful
consideration.

In the first place our manifest desire for reprisals
against Japan and our equally manifest determination to defend against Hitler *for the time being*,
while furnishing unlimited aid to England and
Russia, are a highly important factor in the plan
of the geopoliticians for world domination. For
the Germans have by this time built up an offensive
force — it is really more in the nature of a machine
— that can take care of, crush, capture and absorb
any amount of war material, tanks, planes, guns,
trucks, munitions — as long as that material is used
defensively. And nothing could be better for
Germany *for the time being* than that the products
of American war industry should be expended in
Europe in this way while America is being bled

white by a hopeless Pacific offensive against Japan.

All of this has been incorporated in the latest geopolitical doctrine under the caption of the "Natural Isolation of the United States" which has recently been made an important corollary of the Nazi theory of race. It makes very interesting reading, if only to show how wonderfully thorough the Germans are when they start working on an idea. For both of these theories, the geopolitics of Haushofer and Kjellen as well as the "Racism" of Rosenberg are predicated on the natural or, so to speak, cosmic superiority of the German blood and the German soil, and Germany, the core of the Heart Land, is ethnologically as well as geographically a sort of shrine or holy land of the New Order. Now geographically, the Western Hemisphere and the United States in particular are separated by two great oceans from the holy war which Germany is now raging for possession of the World Island, comprising, as I have said, the continents of Europe, Asia and Africa. And ethnologically the American blood is impure since it contains an admixture of the blood of all races and peoples.

America, therefore, by its position in space is considered to fall outside the Nazi "living room" and also (due to the taint of blood) outside the sacred Nazi culture, being what the geopoliticians call a "satellite island" and thus doomed to eternal spatial and cultural isolation. So that great as we may be in a financial and industrial sense, our role in the future German-controlled world is no different except from the standpoint of size, hours of labor and goods produced than that of Samburan or Madagascar. In short, America is destined to become a sort of Caliban among the nations, a huge misshapen servant of the Nazi Prosperos and Mirandas. Due to our unfortunate isolation, our condition will steadily decline until it is much lower than that of the conquered peoples of Europe since these latter may well be expected to lift their cultural level through association with the German supermen during Chancellor Hitler's next 1000 years.

3

It will be seen from the above that in the Nazi geopolitics, all things work together, if not for good, certainly for the acquisition of space. And with whatever scorn we may regard the ridiculous dialectic with which this claim to dominance is bolstered, it is still impossible to deny the actuality of the German land grabs that have been consummated before our eyes. Since 1935 we have had ample opportunity to observe a technique that for some reason or other seemed to require complicated theories, explanations and ideologies to prepare the way for or to excuse what always turned out to be a cold-blooded steal according to the simple plan: —

> That he shall take who has the power
> And he shall keep who can.

I do not think we were ever fooled for a single moment, but if we were, we should certainly by this time have recognized the utter soullessness and heartlessness of the Nazi space conception. There should not be the shadow of a doubt in the mind of any American that the doctrines of Haushofer and Rosenberg, of Kjellen and Ratsel and List, are utterly materialistic, unnatural, antihuman and at the opposite pole not only from the American Way and the American philosophy of life, but from every one of the great principles which have guided Western Civilization from the Tables of Sinai to the Four Freedoms of the Atlantic Conference.

But at the same time we must also recognize that the practical application of this unholy doctrine in the chapter and verse of German strategy has been unvaryingly successful and that the instrument of this subhuman philosophy of life, the German Army, is spreading like a blight over ever larger portions of the earth's surface. And it should be beginning to dawn upon us that the mere recognition of these truths, which to most of us are now so familiar as to be self-evident, is not enough.

It has now been brought home to us that the Nazi system means war to the death for America and that the only way to win a war is by shooting, that the relentless advance of Germany will continue until it is stopped by the interposition of an insurmountable obstacle. We are, I say, beginning to see these things and the sum total of the practical results of our hardheaded Yankee insight is springing up all around us in the shape of legions of armed men, cantonments, tank and plane assembly lines and the new-laid keels of superdreadnaughts. We lump all of these tangible results of our latest American Dream under the title "National Defense Effort" and we are, there is no denying it, vastly pleased with ourselves on this score. What we do not realize is that this also is not enough.

We think, for example, that all we have to do to stop Hitler is to step up the output of our "defense industry," increase the output of tanks and planes, train more and more flyers ("Keep 'em flying"), induct more and more selectees into our new armies, build an ever increasing number of battleships, spend more and more billions, arm every defending democracy to the teeth, line the pockets of every enemy of Hitler with our gold. It is a process with which we are very familiar, so familiar, in fact, that we think of it as the sign and symbol of America's greatness. We have solved so many problems by increasing the tempo of our industrial machine, by the production and distribution of goods, it is understandable that we should try to solve this one in the same way. But alas! This time it won't work. It is not enough.

We are willing and eager, with an eagerness that is almost pathetic under the circumstances, to tax ourselves heavily, to do without our most cherished luxuries, for the "defense" of America and we are even willing to commit ourselves and our purses to the "defense" of the Western Hemisphere. We say (and we mean it) that we are determined to make the greatest sacrifices to restore the freedom of the seas, enforce the Monroe Doctrine, smite the fifth columnists hip and thigh, hunt down the Communists, keep the Burma Road open, double the lend-lease program, shoot submarines at sight, fight a naval war with Japan. All of which is very, very commendable — only, as I said before, it is not enough.

CHAPTER V

THE SEARCH FOR A FRONTIER

THE AMERICANS of the present generation seem to have forgotten that we are a pioneer people. One reason why we are so opposed to the Nazi space-conception is that this country was settled by men to whom space, even the hostile untamed space of the wilderness, meant freedom. The old European notion that a dynast or autocrat who governs a certain portion of the earth's surface should have absolute control over the inhabitants of that area was repugnant to us and it was due mainly to this repugnance that this nation evolved and became great. From the very beginning, Americans have had their own dreams of geopolitical expansion — they, too, were determined to have their "living room" — only they would have the relation of the individual to the soil he dwells on a relationship of freedom rather than of slavery and they fought the bloodiest war of our history to make their space-conception stick.

There was nothing of the isolationist feather about our pioneer forefathers. They were the greatest interventionists, the biggest land-grabbers of history. They wrested this country from the hostile forces of nature, took it away from the Indians, seized it from the French, the Spanish, the British, dispossessed the slave-holding South, set up the Monroe Doctrine, which Bismarck, forestalling Hitler by half a century, called an "international impertinence" — because it outlawed on an entire hemisphere every other space-conception except their own.

Such a space-conception, once it entered the realm of practical politics, could no more be confined to a given area than the mathematical validity of the symbol *pi* could be confined to a given area, and for the same reason. Neither was a relative, individual or limited thing and both were general, universal and eternal things. *Pi* expressed the relationship between the circumference and diameter of a circle that would be good for any world or set of worlds that imagination could contrive, and the American space-conception expressed a relationship

71

between the individual and the state that was just as eternal as the moral order, because it was based on the moral order and was written in the Ten Commandments and the Sermon on the Mount long before it was written in the Constitution. It was the notion that there are certain basic rights that no earthly power is entitled to invade. The time would come when we would have to fight a "total war" for the luxury of having entertained such a notion, and here again the very universality of our space-conception would help us.

The truth is that the American frontier is always to be found wherever we conceive our space-conception to be threatened and no boundary has ever been set that we would not overrun as long as that threat remained. Today, in order to "defend" that conception against a power that claims the right to world domination, no limit to our operations other than the limits of the habitable globe may be set. The attack on Hitler which is bound to take our armies to Europe is simply the beginning of the tremendous movement of extending the American frontier which is about to begin in the teeth of the most implacable foe that any nation has yet encountered.

The Search for a Frontier

What I am saying is that this nation has always seized its frontiers, not with the idea of defending them but with the idea of extending them so far into the enemy's country as to render that enemy powerless and his threat nonexistent. Of course there was always something to be defended, but it was a thing of the spirit, never a material thing, and the only way to defend it properly was to render its enemies powerless or nonexistent by the ruthless seizure of soil, the relentless attack, the offensive *à outrance*.

Those early settlers of the eighteenth century and those implacable freedom lovers of 1860 knew something that our military experts of today seemed to have forgotten. They knew that in order to defend the American way of life, it is not sufficient merely to defend the soil of America or the material possessions of America, they knew that it is impossible to defend a spiritual thing like freedom or justice from those who would destroy it except by advancing and seizing the territories of the would-be destroyers. If you think about this for a moment you will see why it has to be true.

In fact, the whole tragedy of Europe today is due to the failure of the holders of power in France and England to recognize this until it was too late. They thought that they could draw a line on the earth's surface and say "thus far and no farther." They thought that Western civilization, justice and liberty could flourish on one side of this line and barbarianism on the other. And that was why the initial stages of the Axis attack was a sort of creeping-up process. That is the meaning of the long-drawn-out war of nerves that took place during the period 1935–1939 when the British Empire was stalked by Hitler as an elk is stalked by a panther, when every important outpost on the continent of Europe was taken and occupied by the German Army in preparation for the feral spring against the "line" which France was so determined to defend.

For that is what always happens (and now I am talking plain hardheaded tactics) when one tries to hold a line or a ridge, a bridgehead or a beachhead, a wall or escarpment, and confines one's "defensive effort" to the limits of the area to be defended. If the enemy can take the salient ground to your left or right or center, he can take *you*. It will not be long before your defensive position, no matter with what tenacity you hold it, will prove untenable. No matter what the strength of the garrison may be, it will always be forced to capitulate in the long run if it is merely an army of occupation.

If this is true in tactics, how much more true is it in strategy, in grand strategy? If a company or a regiment must have outposts, if a division needs depth to organize an active defense, if an army must control the terrain to its front before it can feel reasonably safe from the attack of another army, how far forward must we place the advance guard of a continent? Where shall the frontiers of a hemisphere be established in a duel to the death between two such inimical concepts of government as democracy and Hitlerism?

The Romans found the "classic" solution for this problem in their war with Carthage. But let no one suppose that the first successful "defense" plan of history was adopted and put into execution without opposition. There were many politically powerful financiers who openly advocated a "negotiated peace." But in the end, wiser and more heroic counsels prevailed. In the end, with Hannibal's army at the very gates of Rome, it was still possible for the Stern Republic on the Seven Hills to dispatch the expeditionary force which took the war to the enemy and saved the Roman Law and the Roman Justice for eight hundred years.

It was in this fashion that one threat against Western Civilization was dealt with by men who in their daily life as well as in their political concepts were not altogether unlike ourselves. And we must remember that in the year 270 B.C., just before the Punic Wars, these same Romans, later to become the masters of the world, were merely a shrewd, insular, hard-boiled group of merchants and farmers — the Yankees of their epoch — who desired nothing so much as to be let alone and to live at peace with their neighbors.

"Rome," as Lord Bacon truly said, "did not spread upon the world, the world spread upon the Romans." And the truth is that the fight which took the Roman eagles and the Roman frontier to the ends of the earth was in a very real sense a war for self-preservation — exactly the same sort of war, to get down to cases, as we are destined to wage against Germany. Rome's occupation and destruction of Carthage was as much a "defense" measure as Grant's occupation of Richmond or Sherman's destruction of Southern property in Georgia. It was the only way to guarantee the Roman law and the Roman way of life — not only for the time being but for the calculable future of mankind — against a political system uniquely dedicated to its destruction, exactly as Nazism is uniquely dedicated to the destruction of the American constitution and the American way of life.

The Roman space-conception was as firmly rooted to the soil of Italy as ours to the continent of North America but because this conception was a visible dynamic conception (like our own), because (like our own) it related the citizen to his homeland with laws that were considered to be eternal, because the Roman individual from the moment of his birth on Roman soil was considered to be endowed with certain "inalienable" rights which no earthly power was entitled to invade, the Roman space-conception took a lot of defending. It was found very early in the game that it could not be adequately defended simply by mounting guard over the Capitoline Hill and watching the ramparts of Rome.

Now by this time the direction in which this argument is trending should be fairly clear to most readers. And part of that argument is that in dealing with a "total" enemy who wields a "total" threat (i.e. the threat of national extinction) anything short of an all-out offensive is inadequate. There have been peoples like the Babylonians, Egyptians, Assyrians, Chinese, Thebans, Tyrians, French, Russians and British who thought themselves strong and well-fortified, who built walls and ramparts (or ships and tanks and planes) but refused to go out and attack the enemy on his own ground. But such peoples have always paid a tragic and terrible price for their folly.

I do not think that America wants to pay that price for present comfort and a wholly false sense of security. I do not think America can afford to wait behind her "ramparts of ocean" practising "business as usual," amusing herself with defense measures like a god playing with dreams or a child playing with toys, until the enemy has completed his encirclement and is strong enough to attack strategically, or to squeeze economically, always creeping up a little closer, occupying more terrain "under the walls," in order to execute a more decisive attack (or a more comprehensive squeeze) later on.

I do not think that we should wait for this to

happen and perhaps it would help us to make up our minds not to court disaster by waiting if we would glance at the military history of that Western Civilization of which America is now the most powerful representative and whose mantle, for weal or woe, she has, in a manner of speaking, inherited. The Grecian Alexander against the Persians; Rome against Carthage, against Mithridates, against the Gauls; Medieval Europe against the Saracens; Gustavus Adolphus against the Empire that was neither Roman nor Holy; England against Louis XIV, and England again against Napoleon: all illustrate the same point.

Western civilization, law, order and the sense of a calculable future cannot exist with the enemy hovering and skirmishing within bow shot (or bombing range) of the walls. Liberty and the institutions that make for freedom cannot flourish on one side of the fence with tyranny and the institutions that make for servitude grimacing and threatening just across the way. Whenever this has happened to the key nation of the Western tradition, and America is that nation today, there has always been visible a mighty offensive effort. The frontiers of the threatened West have been advanced — advanced in the direction of the threat and far enough to make the civilized life worth living not merely for "our time" but for generations to come.

It is impossible to overestimate the importance of this point to Americans in the present crisis. Its comprehension has been the light and the lodestar of Western strategy from Marathon to the Second Marne. "Do not under any circumstances permit the enemy to reach the walls of the city," wrote Xenophon. "The real frontier of France is at the Brandenburg Gate," said Foch. The principle of war expressed by these two soldiers of the West was one and the same.

Wellington knew it as well as Julius Caesar and it was as perfectly understood (and acted upon) by Lincoln as by Scipio Africanus.

A great part of the meaning of the Crusades, so often ridiculed by historians of the school of Spengler and Haushofer as a vain effort of the mass mind in search of a chimerical goal, lies in the fact that they represented magnificent, if at times wholly unconscious, applications of the principle enunciated above. They were offensives launched against the hostile forces of the East when the East was marshaling a total effort for the destruction of the medieval civilization. It is very evident, moreover, that if the German geopoliticians have the correct idea of the historical process, if a space-conscious, nationally united, dynamic people have a sort of natural right to dominate their epoch, then by every rule of *Weltpolitik* the Janissaries of Achmet II and Suleiman should have held Europe in subjection for at least three centuries.

That this did not happen was due wholly to the offensive effort of the warriors of the West. Medieval Constantinople sat behind its walls without troubling to go out and meet the Mohammedan terror, the Byzantine merchant princes conducted their business as usual and took their profit from Turk and Crusader alike, the garrison of the Maginot Line of the Eastern Empire manned its catapults and ballistae and prepared its pots of "Greek fire" in fancied security, and Constantinople was taken — by Turks who climbed the famous walls with their bare hands or made springboards of their dead to reach the parapets. But the nations of Western Europe were secure because, time and time again, by means of the Crusades, they set their frontiers in the very citadel of the enemy.

The parallel here is so striking as to be worth

dwelling upon at some length, particularly when we consider the question in the light of the recent Japanese attack on our Pacific bases. For Europe had in the centuries between the ninth and fourteenth a situation that bears an almost point-to-point resemblance to the crisis facing America today. With the rise of Islam there appeared upon the stage of Western Civilization a fanatical, military, politically united people with a space-conception which made them seek world domination. Against this group, the medieval counterpart of the totalitarian Axis, there were arrayed the nations of Christendom, with a form of government (feudalism) which divided them politically and made them subject to much internal dissension but with the saving principle that to defend adequately the Faith against the infidel it was necessary to carry fire and sword to his strongholds. It was in this way that the Turk was thrown out of Europe and the frontiers of the West advanced to the Golden Horn.

These attacks on the political and religious framework of the West were all met in the same way, that is to say by a major offensive effort whose first and foremost objective was the extension of the threatened frontier deep into enemy territory.

Faced now with the greatest attack of all history on the institutions of freedom, is it to be supposed that civilization can defend itself some other way? Is it to be supposed that democracy can issue unscathed, if the men of the Western tradition continue to violate the military principle that has proved its efficacy for twenty centuries? For if the men of peace have always managed to overcome the so-called "warrior races," if the men who wanted a calculable future have always defeated and thrown back the aggressors who sought to increase their girths by the destruction of an existing order, there has only been one reason. It happened like this: —

The "warrior races," the Persians, Carthaginians, Mohammedans, Spanish conquistadores, Goths, Visigoths, Huns, the French of Louis XIV and Napoleon, the Germans of 1914, were organized only for attack, expected from their selected victims only defense. Rejoicing in conquest and carnage, sniffing the smoke of battle and crying "Ha ha" among the spears, they said to themselves and to each other: "These Greeks, Romans, medieval city dwellers, are buyers and sellers of goods, whose souls are in their warehouses; these Dutch and

English merchants, these American businessmen, enervated by the slave psychology of Christianity, are the natural, god-given prey of the nations born to the sword." Consequently their surprise and confusion were all the greater when the men of peace launched their victorious attack.

It was all the same old ballyhoo that we are getting today. It was just a way of doing wrong and calling it right to the tune of loud saber rattling; of committing aggressions and then inventing shibboleths to make them stick. But the really peculiar thing about it was that with all the splendor and pomp behind it, with all its armed hosts, big battalions, propagandists, and some very able generals, it always failed to work. It was always crumpled by a well-directed offensive. Every time it came out and glittered and stalked about in the sunshine and made ugly faces it wound up by getting itself knocked on the head and thrown into the dust bin.

2

The Fifth Freedom

That is the way it has always been and that is the way it will be this time unless we are too far gone in sloth and comfort to launch an offensive. And if we fail to do so now we need not wait for Hitler's chains to encompass us, we are already slaves. By the same token, in proportion to our efforts to man and equip and to support an adequate offensive effort, we escape servitude and live to fulfill our destiny as free men.

For leisure — the *otium cum dignitate* of Aristotle — is no longer the prize of the successful businessman or banker, and if we fail to defeat Hitler, economic freedom will be lost forever by every individual alive in the world today. Nor is freedom to be achieved by attending universities and dedicating oneself to the pursuit of the arts and sciences (intellectual freedom); nor as long as Hitler goes unconquered is it to be found in aisles of monasteries or under the domes of temples or in the pulpits and pews of churches or in quiet convent gardens (religious freedom); still less while the battle with Hitler is still to be fought is it to be found in the acts of governors and lawmakers, be they ever so wise and just (political freedom).

Indeed, all of these freedoms, and they are simply the four freedoms of the Atlantic Conference, together with every other freedom we can name, have all come to be united in a single Fifth Freedom which for the time being is the be-all and the end-all of the American nation — the freedom to fight. Thus, while our hands are still untied, our muscles still unbound, our resources still untapped, our independence of action still unfettered, we must use the Fifth Freedom and strike and strike hard in order to end forever the threat to the other four. For as long as that threat persists, no other freedom will have any value whatsoever. In a very real sense, without the fullest exercise of the freedom of the soldier, no one will be able to buy or sell to any advantage, no medium of exchange will retain its value, no frugality or industry will insure the future against want, science and art will go in leading strings, justice will become the mime and buffoon of power-politics, and into what solitude may the contemplative self retire where the raucous voices of our Nazi overlords will not penetrate?

To use this freedom as it should be used means heroism on a gigantic scale and it is precisely this that is now required of us. Shall the Japs be able to gird their loins and practise stern self-denial in order to end our way of life and we be incapable of sacrifice? Shall the Nazis send armies to die in the snows of Russia and on the sands of Africa in order that freedom may perish from the earth while we, the self-styled torch bearers of democracy, are content with an effort limited to the action of our navy and air force in the Pacific? Due to the blind folly and invitational weakness of the past ten years, the price for the defeat of these enemies has been steadily raised until it stands today at a sum as yet unheard of and undreamed of in the annals of military history. What fire and fury of the imagination it took for Hannibal to conceive of the invasion of Italy, what faith was manifested by Saint Louis in launching the Seventh Crusade, what courage animated the heart of Arnold von Winkelried as he rushed upon the Austrian spears at Sempach — all these are mild in comparison with the effort that will be demanded of the nation who shall bring the Axis to book for its crimes.

The price will be high but let us take care in

these last hours that are left, while there is yet light and good works still avail, that it is not made unnecessarily high by further delay and lack of comprehension of the thing to be done and the task to be accomplished. The price is high, so high indeed that of all the nations still unchained America alone has the wherewithal to pay it. And this is simply another reason, if indeed another reason were necessary, why the American effort should be no mere defense project but a spearhead driven with all the strength we can summon straight at the heart of the Nazi Octopus.

CHAPTER VI

A FABLE FOR REALISTS

No ONE can tell the day and the hour when America will make the fateful decision to launch an offensive against Germany and to hurl the accumulative might of three centuries of freedom into the teeth of the pint-pot demigods and mushroom Caesars of the New Europe, but we do know this much: if we are to profit at all by the experiences of our allies, more than a limited offensive is necessary, more than a strategic diversion in the Far East is necessary, more than a naval blockade is necessary, more than the mere occupation of Bermuda or Martinique or Dakar or the mere holding of Manila or Singapore, unless we too like those others, like Poland and France and Belgium and Russia, yes, and like England too, are prepared to pay a really tragic price for experience.

It has always been a mystery to me how from the very beginning of the present discontents, that is to say from the annexation of Austria, which the Archbishop of Canterbury hailed as a "bloodless victory of reason over force," so many prominent people have believed that it was possible to stop Hitler without attacking him. The whole business, and it has been a very miserable business so far, bears more than a superficial resemblance to the ancient Arabian tale of the King's daughter, the potter's son and the pot, *da te fabula.*

There was once a princess whose hand was promised in marriage by the King her father to the suitor, irrespective of rank or age, who could charm the lid from a certain magic pot which had resisted the best efforts of the court magicians. There was the usual dowry of half a kingdom attached to the offer and of course, to make it a really sporting proposition according to the ideas of those times, all unsuccessful contestants were to lose their heads.

It was an age of sorcery, when every monarch practised magic, both black and white, and every potentate maintained his own private retinue of necromancers whose abilities he was prepared to back against all and sundry. So the eligible bachelors, princes and nobles, wealthy commoners and titled fortune hunters, came riding in from the ends of the earth bringing with them a small army of wizards and warlocks. They pitched their tents in the royal courtyard and for weeks on end there was such casting of spells, muttering of incantations, mixing of unholy brews and invoking of evil spirits that a pale-blue light hung over the palace and the air fairly rustled with unseen presences — but the obstinate lid refused to budge and the King's executioner collected a small fortune in head taxes every week end.

And then there came a potter's son who happened to be passing through town on his lawful occasions and demanded to know what all the excitement was about. Being told, he desired to try his luck and after some wrangling with the court chamberlain over his identification papers he was finally ushered into the dread chamber where the magic pot stood, piled high, so the story goes, with the tails of small devils and slippery with the blood of toads that had been sacrificed upon it. It was a gruesome place by all accounts but our potter's son was a realist. "A pot is only a pot," he said reassuringly to himself, "and who should know that better than a potter's son." With these words he reached out valiantly and, grasping the lid with both hands (for it was a very large pot), lifted it off.

A pot is only a pot; a war is only a war. One opens the one by lifting the lid off and one wins the other by advancing upon the enemy, seizing his lands, castles, forts and treasures and driving him forth from his strongholds.

Now from time immemorial, in order to accomplish this, it has been necessary to attack. Up to now, as far as the democracies are concerned, this has been, in very truth, a phony war, and the reason is that the classic maxim of strategy, the principle that has been successfully followed by every great captain from Joshua to Foch, the categorical imperative of successful generalship — seek out the enemy's masses and attack them — has been consistently neglected.

There has always appeared to be a good reason for this conduct of war, so to speak, by indirection or on the oblique and a thousand methods of beating Hitler without attacking him have been suggested by a thousand different experts. Let us note, however, that the war efforts of the democracies, thus far, have been characterized by one or more of three cardinal mistakes which grew out of the violation of this ancient strategic principle. For either they have been (1) purely defensive in a very narrow tactical sense and have been overcome by the enemy's offensive effort, or (2) where there have been technical offensives they were too weakly launched, or (3) they have been indirect and they have been aimed at an accessory rather than at the main objective which, as Napoleon pointed out, must always be the "masses of the enemy."

Liddell Hart, adumbrating the Mahan thesis of sea supremacy, started this theory of indirection in strategy as a sort of corollary to his doctrine of limited liability, the idea behind the whole thing being that an enemy can be defeated in some other way besides attacking him and a war can be won in some other way besides fighting it. In one remarkable passage, he mentions with gusto the fact that Turenne and de Montecuccoli consumed two campaigns without fighting a single battle. Right along with this concept, which has been a Godsend to Hitler in his triumphal march across Europe, goes the notion that old-fashioned generalship is in the decline and that the wars of the future will be won by technicians employing the highly complicated machine placed at their disposal by modern industries. The Maginot Line was such a machine, the British fleet is another and, at the present writing, there seems to be some division of opinion among the experts as to whether Hitler is destined to be crushed by the product of the American plane factories or by our two-ocean navy ready by 1944.

It is a mistake to suppose that these false ideas have been wholly discredited by the German victories. Notions so much in accordance with the weaknesses, the sloth and the easy, wishful thinking of the democracies do not so readily yield their power over the minds of men. Some authorities have fallen from their high estate but others are still voicing their expert opinions; others explain with irrefutable logic why it is that we should cut our army down to the bare minimum necessary for defense and increase lend-lease spending to the maximum. Some are still talking about the natural protection of two oceans and it has been stated recently at great pains that to beat Hitler all we need is lots of giant bombers; and newspapers, not content with publishing the opinions of these pundits in their columns, have become so enamored of these new versions of "the indirect attack" and "limited liability" (for that is all they are) that just before the Japanese attack on Pearl Harbor they were placing them unconsciously in their very headlines: —

AMERICAN TANKS CONQUER IN LIBYA
AMERICAN PLANES DOWN NAZI FLYERS

What does all this mean except that a lot of us believe, and take delight in believing, that the product of our factories, without generalship, without an American expeditionary force or an American battle, will be able to defeat Hitler. For some reason or other this is called "realism." But this is the age-old tragic fallacy of the supreme weapon, the weapon that will do the trick without fighting and without risk to the fortunate nation who possesses it and can go into the mass production necessary to overwhelm the enemy with it. It should be plain by this time that wars are not won that way, that from the Hannibalic elephants that failed signally to make the Carthaginian campaign a pushover through all the gadgets and war chariots of the Middle Ages down to the introduction of poison gas by the Germans in 1916, war is won not by machines alone and not by men alone, but by a dexterous combination of the two given direction by generalship that is willing to take the inescapable risk.

2

It has been said that Hitler owes a great part of his success to his careful selection of objectives which to the minds of the conservative statesmen and generals of Europe were definitely in the realm of the "improbable." But the truth is, and we may as well face it, that practically every goal he declared in advance in *Mein Kampf*, every campaign he planned, every victory he won, from his first seizure of power in Germany to his last seizure of oil in Rumania, has been, according to our old way of thinking, an improbability so remote that it approached the impossible. The reason why the things we said couldn't happen have happened, and the victorious conquests and enslavements we thought couldn't possibly occur have occurred, is due largely to our ideas of what is probable and what is improbable in the war that we are now waging.

A Fable for Realists

It is high time we changed our notions in this respect also. It is high time for us to realize that concepts of what is probable or improbable in war and politics, derived from the limited navy-dominated national conflicts of the nineteenth century, are not only misleading but downright dangerous when used in connection with the unlimited continental warfare (a combination of strategy and politics) now being waged by Hitler. Our concepts are the tools by which we grasp reality but here we have a set of realities entirely new to our experience — a group of values (military and political) which elude our every effort to estimate them correctly. Obviously our concepts need revision.

Of course, statesmen and generals have to deal in probabilities, and the knack of grasping and separating mentally the probable from the improbable, discarding the one and using the other, is the very life blood of successful statesmanship as it is of successful strategy. This is precisely what has made Hitler victorious thus far: that he has been able to see that what his enemies, the defense-thinking, fleet-bound democracies, regarded as improbable, according to the old method of limited warfare, was so probable as to be within the realm of certainty if one unleashed one's ideas and dared to think offensive strategy in terms of the new streamlined methods of total warfare.

According to the concepts adopted by Hitler from the very beginning (a good many of them have been cashed in the coin of reality since), if one adopted offensive strategy on a total scale one immediately got out of the realm in which operations were limited by things that couldn't be done because (a) they had never been done before (practical improbabilities) or (b) civilized human beings simply didn't do such things (ethical improbabilities) into a realm in which the sky was the limit and one was perfectly free to try anything at least once. Once in this region, it would not really matter whether you were dealing with the administration and officer personnel of the German Army or the administration and political personnel of the German Reich. It didn't matter whether you were thinking of the use of armies or the use of weapons or whether you were dreaming specifications for a new armored vehicle or going into a trance to get the outline of a new blitzkrieg; as long as your concept of the probability of a favorable outcome was based on unlimited offensive warfare and as long as the rest of the world plodded along with its conservative defensive estimates of the probable and the possible, your dice would be loaded, your cards were stacked ready to your hand and no matter whether you did make a few mistakes, it would be very difficult indeed for you to lose in the long run.

This, then, is the one and only key to the so-called astounding and unbelievable success of Hitler and it might be well to review briefly his employment of it in his handling of the German Army. With this idea in view, he would purge his officer corps and weed out the old Prussian martinets, replacing them with men like Guderian who were wedded to the offensive. The author will never forget the howl of derision which rose from the ranks of American and British military conservatives and made its appearance in the service journals of both nations at this so-called Nazification of the old tried-and-true German Army. It was confidently held that the German military class had been betrayed by a visionary who happened to hold political power and that the German Army would never regain its former discipline and efficiency.

To understand the deeper meaning of this reform of an army with offensive strategy in mind, compare the now well-known French and British difficulties in the matter of relieving inefficient officers and our own Congressional outcry over the relief of certain over-age National Guard generals after the maneuvers last fall. By doing this we are enabled to get some idea of the width and depth of the abyss that separates total military concepts of the Hitleresque variety from the futility and frustrations that hamper the democracies. One might well ask: are we, the most resourceful nation on earth, going to resign ourselves to trailing Hitler in this matter of administration? Then we are defeated before we start, for the simple reason that the offensive or total method of conducting operations refuses to tie itself down to any stereotyped procedure or any infallible group.

Exactly the same thing goes for the new tactics where the methods that are used and found successful in one war, and are slavishly imitated by potential enemies industrially preparing for *their* chance "to beat the champ," are unhesitatingly

scrapped by Hitler in favor of new and as yet untried techniques developed, apparently, extempo-
raneously. And in the same way adaptations are
made which are uniquely suited to the terrain and
to the nature of the mission. For in offensive total
warfare, as waged by Hitler, there is no limit except
the necessary one of the objective. Such a war is
always fought with tactical and strategical devices
that always surprise the enemy who is always
trailing and always comes out second best. It is
worth while dwelling on this point at some length
because it is vital for America and for the world
that we should see, and understand fully, the
reason for the German success.

The invasion of Norway bears little resemblance
to the invasion of Belgium and the mountainous
warfare of the Balkans is conducted on an entirely different model from the attack on the
Maginot Line. In Poland, for example, the Germans used armored "fingers" which forged ahead,
detouring obstacles with apparent indifference to
lines of communication and supply. And so when
the prompter's bell rang for the Russian campaign,
the armies of Stalin, confidently expecting that the
same tactics would be used, made complete prepara-

tions for a defense *in mass* that could not be detoured or sidestepped, and which, so Timoshenko calculated, would inevitably result in Bock being cut off from his bases after the first battle. But the Germans, understanding well the meaning of the Russian masses in a war where the space factor was of secondary consideration (Napoleon regarded it as primary — and was defeated), abandoned the armored *finger* in favor of the armored *whip* which, after going so far, turned back and made a loop. The "wedge and kessel" tactics which resulted from this bold improvisation spelled disaster for the defenders whose mass formations only served to make their capture (or destruction) more certain.

3

In the success of the German operations during the past two years, we can find, if we will only look, lesson after lesson in the superiority which offensive methods of strategy and tactics are able to achieve because of the *freedom* which these methods give the attacker in the selection of objectives and, when the objective has been selected, we see the blow carefully timed and prepared as regards direction and scope. Thus the movement of armies (strategy), the design and use of weapons (tactics), the making of treaties, the organization of espionage, formation of fifth columns, study of geography, regimentation of labor and industry — all are considered in an absolute sense with one single dominating idea in view — conquest.

For it is evident that the offensive, in the sense that we are now considering it, will not be bound by any limitations of space or time, or by what used to be called at our War College "economy of effort." It will take risks that, according to our nineteenth-century, or First World War, military concepts, appear staggering, but which, when one considers the mentality of the "defenders," are no risks at all. In fact, the laws governing momentum and inertia being what they are, the offensive, or absolute, war is bound to win as long as it encounters nothing more dynamic than defensive or limited military systems.

We can thus see a system of warfare in operation that has an *infinitude* of means at its disposal for the employment of the supreme act of force in battle. And conversely, we may see how the "defensive" system of the Allies, France and England and, later, Russia, first as regards strategy is doomed from the start to take a passive role, voluntarily throwing away the initiative because of preconceptions; next, as regards tactics, when the actual moment of battle arrives and the armies are in furious combat, we can see very plainly, if we will only look, how this same "defensive" system imposes its tragic limitations on the use of weapons.

I have already pointed out in a previous chapter how devotion to what the old-school tacticians called the principle of the reserve prevented Corap's attacking immediately after the Sedan breakthrough, thus giving von Kleist time to build up that fatal salient which was to pierce the heart of France. But this is only an example among many of the handicaps with which the defense concepts so burdened the Allied generals until, in their actual use of the armed force at their disposal, the weapon always seemed too heavy for the hand that held it.

But in the case of Hitler, who wages warfare according to the offensive, absolute or total model, each campaign is prepared with meticulous care in order that the maximum of force may be brought to bear on a predetermined enemy with full consideration given to those two other strategic variables, the time and space factors. The blueprint having been made, the news reel of Nazi conflict unfolds and in each case the astonished conservatives and "defense thinkers" of neighboring countries see what appears to be a new and unbelievably daring use of military and political power.

In the Polish campaign, Hitler does not scruple to make a complete *volte face* from his previously anti-Comintern position in order to gain the temporary neutrality of Russia. Since time is a cardinal factor here, his armies advance across Poland in rapidly moving, well-extended fingers in complete disregard of reserves, lines of communication and supply. It was thought by the military "realists" of England, France and America that the Polish Army, considered one of the finest in Europe, would hold the Germans enmeshed for at least a year. It was thought, moreover, that any sort of an agreement, gentlemen's or otherwise, between Hitler and Stalin was an impossibility. And finally, when the impossibility became a *fait accompli*, it was thought that Russia was only waiting for a propitious moment of the campaign to strike her deadly enemy in the flank. But in this, the first military campaign of Nazism against the defense thinkers of the European democracies, the realists were to learn a good many lessons in the conduct of war.

In many respects, Hitler's Polish campaign resembled Napoleon's first campaign in Italy where the Austrians criticized the French tactics even as they fled precipitately from the fire power of the French skirmishers. In both cases, a new method of war was being unfolded, or if not a "new" method, a method that had long been untried. In both cases, there was the same extravagant use of the armed force, the same recklessness as regards casualties, the same operations on "interior lines," the same penetrations, the same concentration on mobility at the expense of lines of communication. But in the end, when it was all over and Poland lay prostrate after a four-weeks campaign that had left the German military machine without a dent, it was all explained away by the realists. The success of the German air squadrons in destroying the Polish hangars, the disaster which followed in the wake of the German dive bombers' destroying the

Polish supply bases, was all attributed to the lack of fast attack planes in the Polish Army.

Did anyone in the French Army, General Corap for example, stop to think that these dive bombers which were used so successfully against the Polish hangars might be used with equal success against French artillery or infantry? In the same way, and in accordance with the same sort of thinking, the success of the Nazi tanks in the Polish campaign was attributed to the lack of antitank guns by the Poles, and the success of the German engineers in blowing up bridges and railroads was held to be due to traitors and fifth columnists in the Polish ranks.

But if we study this picture carefully, we can get a very clear idea, and for America, a very salutary idea, of how the defense mind works in *tactics* (we have already seen it at work in strategy). In the case before us, the basic or guiding idea is the notion of order, of symmetry on the battle-field. It is the notion that there is a sort of metaphysical, one-to-one correspondence between weapons of offense and weapons of defense and that symmetrical relationship must always hold good. Thus to counter the relatively slow-moving bomber, which you assume will only be used against fixed ground installations such as aerodromes, railroad yards or supply centers, you have the fast attack planes; against the tank you have the anti-tank gun; against attacking infantry, you have defending infantry and reserves; against attacking artillery, you have counter-battery artillery. There are lines, fortifications, barriers, which you assume cannot be taken, and in the last analysis when the enemy penetrates these, there is always that good old stand-by, the "defense in depth."

Thus, after the Maginot Line was cracked and Weygand replaced Gamelin as commander-in-chief, a sort of universal cry of warning and of hope went up from the defense thinkers in France and England as well as from the American "armchair strategists": *Defend in depth! Stabilize the front! Employ antitank guns* — the famous French 75's firing direct fire on German *Panzer* columns!

These were the magic words heard everywhere during that fatal week of May 1940, as the democratic world sat back to watch the outcome of the duel to the death between the disciple of Foch and the German tacticians. We all know what happened but I wonder if we know how it happened.

A Fable for Realists

We all know that Weygand never had a Chinaman's chance to stem the tide of a German invasion but I wonder if we know why. And I wonder most of all, if knowing, we are willing, even at this late date, to apply the knowledge gained to our own concept of tactics.

For if one thing stands out clearly in the battle that Weygand and von Brauchitsch fought out to a finish it is the tremendous limitations that defense tactics impose on the defenders, and the almost infinite opportunity that is offered the resourcefulness and ingenuity of the attacker in exploiting any initial success gained by his careful planning and superior momentum. The Germans broke through at Sedan because their offensive strategy was unlimited by any hypothesis or preconception of invulnerability in the selection of strategic direction, that of the Ardennes, which the French general staff "decided" was impassable. They had selected the Sedan hinge for the application of their wedge without thought of communication, supply or reserves (mobility would soon rectify *that* disadvantage) and simply and solely for strategic reasons, i.e. through there they could best drive a barrier of steel between the British and French, thrusting the former into the sea and settling the hash of the latter afterwards.

Now do you suppose the French and British (and American experts with the French and British Armies) didn't see the advantages of this sort of plan? Of course they did. They had been talking about it, writing about it, lecturing about it for twenty years, but they didn't believe it. Like the Pharisees in the Bible, who didn't believe in our Lord even when he raised Lazarus from the tomb, the staff mentality wasn't going to believe in something or react to something that it had decided in advance was impossible. The staff mentality with its defense concepts of the three strategic variables of time, space and force, had decided in advance that the German thrust was coming from the north. It was coming from the north because Plan XIV said so, because only a "visionary," i.e. only an offensive, strategist would so neglect the opportunities of terrain gently sloping downward, easy access to supply bases, short lines of communication, which advance over the Belgian plain would give the attacker.

They would not believe in an attack from the flank and even when they had unimpeachable evidence that it was coming, they still did not believe it, but continued to move their armies northwards in accordance with the defense myth. Then, when the attack occurred and was successful, when the awful, agonizing penetration of France began, they sprang once more to the defense.

Is the sole means by which the disaster could have been averted ever adopted? Is a counterattack launched? Does the leopard change its spots? No, not even at the last trump do the defense-minded staff intellects adopt the offensive. Once more refuge is taken in a preconception. Another hypothesis is coined, "the front must be stabilized — we shall defend in great depth," so the French armies will roll out the 75's, every foot of ground between the Meuse and Paris will be defended by gunners aiming their field pieces right at the German tanks. The 75's, well-concealed, holding their fire until the enemy shows the whites of his eyes, will be manned by French gunners who will die in their tracks rather than yield an inch of the soil of *La Patrie*. Defense in depth, that is the answer to tanks; stabilize the front, dig trenches, mine roads, blow up bridges, *stabilize the front*.

Stabilize, depth, anti-tank defense — these are

blind words! Blind words that make the democratic world breathe more easily. No one supposed that the German advance in France would be any different from German advance in Poland in long, tenuous fingers of armored columns, completely cut off from each other by the heavily forested terrain (an advance through defiles); no one supposed that where Bock and von Runsted had extended and lengthened their armored forces for the conquest of Poland, von Brauchitsch would mass, concentrate, and foreshorten his tank masses for the conquest of France.

The very victory which gave the German tacticians the greatest latitude in the selection of the tactical means to be used in the offensive severely limited the French in their selection of the tactical means of defense. The lessons of the Polish campaign were learned all right, but they were learned — as such lessons have always been learned and always will be learned by the staff mentality — too late and they were learned all wrong.

It was because of the inevitable preconceptions of staff thinking that the antitank defense in depth was made to depend on direct fire of 75 mm. guns.

A Fable for Realists

We know now what actually did happen when the heavily armored *Panzer* columns made contact with these wholly inadequate defenses. Of course it has been held by many critics that, given the weight and impetus of the German attack and the inferiority of the French armored vehicles (everybody is quite certain of the inferiority of the French vehicles), the German victory was assured from the start. It has also been argued *ad nauseam* that in the face of the rapidity of the German advance, no counteroffensive was possible. Nothing could be further from the truth. A great army does not go down so easily as all that, unless, as was actually the case here, its assets, i.e. its "offensive potential," are frozen by a false concept. What is necessary is first of all that the high command and staff of an army should be able to think offensively. But to think offensively, with any hope of success, one must think rapidly and translate the thought into dispositions, expedients, maneuvers which will import the element of surprise into the operations. As I have already pointed out, it is to do what the enemy least expects.

Now in the German advance into France, to come back to specific cases, the French used tanks against tanks and the Germans, expecting this, countered the French light tanks with medium tanks and the medium (French) tanks with heavy tanks; the French used the light 37 mm. rapid-firing antitank gun against the spearheads of the German armored divisions but the Germans knew this in advance and placed their heaviest armored vehicles in the van with the result that the light French guns were wiped out as soon as they disclosed their locations by fire. Then the French sought to organize a position-defense in depth but the Germans, expecting this also, since they had the French theory of defense warfare at their finger tips, so maneuvered their armored columns that the French 75 mm. guns which were heavy enough for the mission assigned, if the enemy had obligingly launched the sort of attack expected of him, were destroyed by tanks coming up on the flanks and rear while adjusting on targets to the front. This pitiful sacrifice of brave men and matériel which would have been wholly adequate if used properly continued throughout the Battle of France. It will probably rankle forever in the breasts of Frenchmen alongside of "the accursed memory of Waterloo" — only, unlike Waterloo, it was quite unnecessary.

Such are the truths which a realistic view of the military operations in Europe during the past two years must emphasize. We turn now to the application of these lessons to the situation facing America as she wades deeper and deeper into the greatest war of history.

CHAPTER VII

THE LESSON OF MANILA
AND SINGAPORE

IT HAS been hard for the American people to watch the fall of the Philippines under the never-ceasing erosion of the Japanese attacks, and it is harder still to recognize (as we must if we have not lost our sense of reality) that General MacArthur and the brave men fighting under him were doomed to defeat from the start. But if we will take heed in time, if we will learn the lesson which this sacrifice holds for us, the loss not only of the islands themselves, but even of the brave men who fought and died there for an utterly mistaken concept of strategy, will not have been in vain.

Now the lesson of the Philippines (and of Hong Kong, and Singapore) is simply this: continental warfare being what it is, particularly as regards the decisive tactical value of land-based aircraft, it is impossible to hold any possession, island or base, by a defense whose principal buttress is an existing sea supremacy. Unless the foundations of victory are laid by the formation of an adequate land army — not a garrison or a "defense force" — mere sea power, however great its supremacy over the enemy may be, is useless except for rescue work. What this means, translated into terms of today's Pacific tragedy, is that the decision to hold the Philippines against a possible Japanese attack (and anyone who had reached the age of reason by 1931 should have known that a Japanese attack was possible) should not have been made last month or last year, it should have been made ten years ago when Japan, by starting her invasion of Manchukuo, gave us the high sign that she was in the way to become an "aggressor nation."

The day of that invasion was the dead-line date when we should have made our decision either to hold or to abandon the Philippines as a military and naval base. If we had decided to hold, we should have then and there come down on Japan like a ton of bricks. That was the time for us to have gained a real continental foothold (rather than an island perch) in the Far East. It might have meant, and very probably would have meant, a tidy little war with Japan which we could easily have won then. It might have meant and very probably would have meant establishing a protectorate over China, going all out for the industrial development of that country, including the construction of airplane factories and military airports all over the Orient as well as the building up of reserves of strategic raw materials in Chinese continental bases — all of which could easily have been done then; it might have meant keeping a sizable army of at least 200,000 men in China, which would have been worth a good deal more than the cost of its upkeep as a stabilizing factor in the Far East.

But if we were not willing to do any of these things, if every single one of them seemed preposterous, then we should have abandoned the idea of holding the Philippines, for we should have known that without a real continental base in Asia, the military position of the United States in the Far East was absolutely untenable. You can have it one way or you can have it the other way but if you try to have it both ways you will simply be condemning the brave men of your defending garrison to certain defeat or to equally certain death, and that is what our abysmal foolishness, our blowing hot and blowing cold, eating our cake and keeping it, has done in the Philippines.

It is cold comfort to know that we are not alone in our woe, that our ally, Britain, has paid for the last two years, and is still paying heavily, for her devotion to the sea-power concept. But it is none the less true that in this respect, I mean as regards brave men sacrificed uselessly, wasteful expenditure of wealth and material and loss of prestige to ourselves and corresponding gain to the enemy, the lesson of Manila is no different from the lessons of Narvik and Greece and no different except in degree of arrant foolishness displayed from the lesson of Dunkirk. For where Britain failed in the Far East because her continental land army was practically nonexistent, she has failed thus far in Europe because that army was always too weak as regards the task assigned, and the force at the enemy's disposal, to launch a decisive offensive.

And with this word "decisive," the cat is out of the bag. For decisiveness in battle connotes the disposal of really important land forces and this the democracies have as yet been unwilling to do because of the risk involved. So they are all, America as well as England, clinging like grim death to the outworn, outdated notion that a base perched on some cape or promontory, dominating some passage or estuary and supported and supplied by sea, can be maintained in the face of an enemy who has achieved continental supremacy.

This is the reason why the British expeditionary forces dispatched to France in 1939, to Norway in 1940, to Greece in 1941, have always been too small to launch a real continental offensive and the pitiless logic of battle soon demonstrated their utter uselessness. For all the good they did they might as well have been kept at home to furnish details for the Buckingham Palace guard mount or for the sentry posts on Whitehall Street. And what is true of these armies that were sent to certain defeat on the continent of Europe is even more true of the forces in Singapore and Manila. Commentators may rend their garments and call the gods to witness that Singapore must be held and our military experts may show conclusively, and beyond peradventure of a doubt, that Luzon will never be taken by the Japanese. But both Singapore and Luzon, like Hong Kong and Guam, must fall. They must fall because they cannot be held without offensive land power, and this is precisely what the peoples concerned were unwilling to risk.

It has been a hard lesson but let us hope that at long last, we have learned it; let us now, by all means, draw the sword and throw away the scabbard, but as we advance, let us be committing to memory the following principles which govern the continental total war now being waged over the entire earth: (1) sea power is indecisive without land power; (2) defensive land power is doomed; (3) offensive land power is only to be gained by the disposal of major forces, including air forces, in a continental theater.

2

Here we reach the second, and prescriptive, part of the lesson of Manila. In the light of this knowledge so tragically gained of the things we should not have done in the past, we may direct our efforts towards the task that is still to be accomplished. The sudden, treacherous, and deadly attack of Japan has simply outlined that task more clearly, placing in bolder relief the immutable laws that govern successful warfare. We must launch a major offensive in Europe. We must strike at Adolf Hitler. On no account must we let the war with Japan deflect us from our central purpose or weaken our main effort.

Thus, from the lesson of Manila, must spring a series of military acts that will be in every sense more absolute, more relentless, more determined in their search for power than anything Hitler has yet been able to devise. It may be necessary for us to make sacrifices undreamed of by our heroic forefathers, it may be necessary to launch two expeditionary forces, prepare two offensives, one directed at Asia, the other at Europe — but we must always keep in mind that no matter how strong we make the former, its strength should never be comparable to the latter and we must never forget that the weakening of our effort in the Atlantic theater, and the confusion of our opinion as regards the war against Germany, has been an object of constant effort and planning on the part of Hitler. To this end was the Japanese attack launched on the Pacific bases, nor can there be any doubt that considering the whole picture from Hitler's standpoint and keeping in mind the dangerous position in which he found himself, it was launched in the nick of time.

In this order of ideas, the Japanese attack on Pearl Harbor from the standpoint of the Axis was a forlorn hope. This attack must therefore be regarded, not as the insolent gesture of an enemy who believed victory to be within his grasp, but as the last throw of the dice of a gambler who has staked his shirt. For Japan, gutted by a decade of war, suffering from economic strangulation, wholly possessed by the eviscerating demon of militarism, has no other chance for survival except in sharing the spoils won by a victorious Germany. Therefore, her future must, by the inescapable necessity of the last ten years, be in the hands of Hitler and she is now, in a very real sense, the tool and the vassal of Germany and must do the bidding of her overlord or face certain extinction.

And by the same token, Germany, bled white by the losses of the Russian campaign, facing the coming winter with her armies still short of their goal, and with the ground under her feet beginning to tremble with revolution, was under the same sort of necessity as Japan. She had to do something that would avert her doom. At this critical moment, the most critical of the entire war, an American attack on Germany would have spelled disaster. Therefore, something must be done to avoid it. America must become so heavily engaged in the Orient that her vast resources of man power and munitions would flow in the opposite direction *for a while*. Japan, Germany's vassal state, was therefore ordered to advance into the breach and there was nothing left for her to do but obey.

Moreover, in estimating the reasons that lay behind the attack of December 7, 1941, we must never lose sight of the fact that since 1939, Germany has never had to cope with two major antagonists on land at the same time. Never have the democracies succeeded in establishing a second front, never has Hitler had to change his carefully prepared plan of attack in order to guard his flanks and rear against an offensive launched by his enemies.

If you will consider a moment, you will see the importance of this point in connection with the Japanese attack on the United States. Hitler was bogged down in Russia, his plans had miscarried by at least six months and, according to his calculations, the final kill would have to wait until spring. By that time, his enemies could build a new front against him in the Near East and perhaps in the Ukraine. That front would be built during the winter with American help in ships, planes and tanks and by the time the snows melted in the North, it would be manned with American troops to whom the winter of 1941–1942 would have given the polish and final battle training necessary for launching them at the German *Panzer* Divisions. That would have been the reasonable thing for America to do, that would have been the way the situation should have been handled. There, in the first miscarriage of the "Great Calculator's" plans, lay the golden opportunity of his enemies to win the war; to build up a second front during the winter when the mass of the German armies around Moscow and Leningrad dare not move without the danger of having the savage Russians at their throat, build it up while Atlantic sea lanes are still open, using the combined navies and air forces of America and England to guard the convoys, *and in the spring*, the real democratic offensive.

That was what Hitler himself would have done and if it were done with sufficient energy and resolution, things being what they were in Europe (as nobody knew better than Hitler himself), the game was up. There was only one hope. America must be made to face the Orient until the Russian *coup de grâce* could be administered, American indignation must be so aroused, American wrath so stirred that the major American effort would be directed toward Japan rather than toward Germany. For this reason, it would not be sufficient for the little brown brothers merely to declare war or even to indulge in their favorite pastime of an undeclared war against the United States. An act combining to a high degree the ferocity and treachery that are so loathsome to the American soul must be carefully planned and perpetrated at exactly the right moment, not only for its actual practical success in the selected theater of war but for its effect (call it propaganda effect) on the public opinion of America. These are the main reasons for the savage attack on Luzon and Oahu while transpacific affairs were being arbitrated in council — an attack so timed that it reached the ears of the American people while the revered and beloved head of our Department of State was actually in conference with Japanese envoys.

I have spoken above of the long fight which Western Civilization waged in the Middle Ages with another Eastern people, the Mohammedans, but it is necessary to point out that the attack of December 7, 1941, was not strictly speaking "Eastern" in any sense of the word — no follower of Mohammed, no paynim sons of swarthy Spain, ever conceived such an act of bottomless treachery, nor do I believe that the Japanese themselves, for all their well-earned reputation for infamy, could alone have achieved it. For it bears all the earmarks of its author, Adolf Hitler. It is, without the slightest doubt, the unique production of that same malevolent genius who engineered the land grabs of 1937, 1938 and 1939, and who, as *advocatus diaboli* of the Western world, is past, pluperfect, prestissimo player of the game of international perfidy invented by Machiavelli.

No! — the Pacific air and sea attack was not a Japanese thing; it was a German thing, prepared by Germans, ordered by Germans, and to a large extent executed by Germans; and the author, instigator and executor of this bloody pseudo-Oriental high-jinks was the grand Nazi mumbo-jumbo, who sits smirking modestly behind his mustache in Berchtesgaden, watching with complacency, and quite understandable relief, the mounting American indignation against Japan. He rightly calculated in the beginning and finally managed to convince Japan towards the end (or she never would have become his cat's-paw). If this keeps up he is safe. Germany is safe and, believe it or not, so is Japan.

3

It is an adult, not a childish attitude that is demanded of us by this Japanese situation. We are dealing with an Oriental people, a people whose policies towards the West are formulated slowly, whose decisions crawl always on all fours, the known to the known — never flying, as ours do sometimes, from the known to the unknown. For a long time, the Japanese have watched Hitler forging the chains for a Europe which the democratic guardians of freedom seemed unable to protect. For a long time, they have seen every foe of Hitler to whom Britain had promised protection, France, Norway, Belgium, Poland, Greece, go under almost as soon as the British promise of armed assistance was given. Japan has also watched closely the reactions of the United States as she continued her course of treaty breaking and aggression in China, and nothing that she saw led her to believe that we were ready to undertake a war in the Pacific.

Now, in the simplicity of the Japanese mind, it was reasonable to suppose *first*, that Hitler was able to protect his friends and smite his enemies; *second*, that England could be safely left out of the reckoning since she was so tied down to the defense of the British Isles that she was negligible as an opponent either in Europe or in the Far East; *third*, that the United States was unwilling to attack the Axis in Europe but would confine her efforts in that direction to lend-lease; *fourth*, that the United States was unable, considering her commitments to England in the manner of war materials and supplies, to launch the sort of offensive in the Pacific which would be successful against Japan.

Of these four propositions to which, after ten years of careful experimentation in the matter of aggression, the Japanese mind assented, only one was true, to wit: that the United States was unable for the time being to launch a successful offensive in the Pacific theater of operations without stemming the tide of her assistance to England in the Atlantic theater of operations. That is to say, for the time being — considering the spaces involved (six thousand miles of ocean), the lack of naval repair bases (Singapore was doomed), the impossibility of establishing land-based aviation in the western Pacific (the Philippines could not hold out a month) and most important of all, the lack of a continental foothold (which America should have secured in China but had not) — Japan was safe.

But with Hitler in the saddle in Europe and the only power able to unseat him committed to a hopeless offensive in the Pacific, to be safe for the time being was to be safe forever. It was to win the war. Therefore, so the Japanese argument continued — a true conclusion drawn from false premises — let the United States attack in the Pacific — the stronger her attack the better the chance Hitler has this crucial spring of being victorious over Russia and England. And with Germany supreme in Europe, with Germany able to mobilize the strength of Europe against America's Atlantic seaboard, the Pacific supremacy desired by the Japanese immediately becomes a reality.

It should be clear now that Hitler and his Japanese ally are simply duplicating over a vastly greater area, and with tremendously increased potentialities for good or evil, the same grand strategy that worked so well in the squeeze-play executed against France in the spring of 1940. It is a favorite trick of Hitler's (he did the same thing in the Balkan campaign of 1941 with Greece and Turkey) and if we have not utterly lost the hindsight of our Yankee ancestors, it should not deceive us for one moment. In the case of France, it was Mussolini's anticipated declaration of war that kept two million French soldiers on the Italian border and out of the decisive battle of the North until it was too late to use them effectively. In our own case, it is the reality of a Japanese attack on our Pacific bases that is counted on to freeze the fighting strength of the United States in the Pacific theater until it is too late. In the case of France, it was the Maginot Line that was counted upon to hold in the North and center until the French Army of the South chastised the insolence of the treacherous Italians. In the case of the United States, a veritable barrage of propaganda was loosed, coincident with the invasion of Luzon, to make us believe that the Germans were on the run in Europe and that Russia could deal adequately with them while America, aided by England, launched a punitive expedition against the treacherous Japanese.

Indeed, the parallel can be carried a good deal farther and it can be shown that it was political influence, plus a nationwide emotional reaction, keyed to highest pitch by the fear of losing Corsica and Nice to the Italian banditti, that tied Weygand's hands in respect to the use of forces which might have been decisive had they been used in time. Alas! In the end, it was not only Corsica and the Mediterranean coast that was lost, but all France. Now is it not our own fear of losing our Pacific bases plus the fear of a Japanese invasion of California that is causing us to turn our eyes and deflect our strength towards the Pacific?

We must be warned in time, we must beware of this enemy who desires to direct our attention from his point of weakness to his position of greatest strength, this enemy who is even now making a desperate effort to convince us that we should not strike him in the one place where he is quite unable to defend himself. If we do this, if we turn westwards with our main effort, we shall be doing exactly what Hitler wants us to do, but if we are warned in time, if we can bring ourselves to see reality in its true perspective, it is not too late to upset his calculations by an Atlantic offensive launched with all the fire and fury of Gettysburg.

CHAPTER VIII

THE REVERSAL OF HISTORY

WHAT HITLER has done is to establish three circles, not by any means concentric as some writers have seemed to indicate, but intersecting in such a way that there is one area common to all; and that area is the sphere of dominating influence, the Heart Land of the geopoliticians — Nazi Germany. If we superimpose the three circles, each one representing the sphere of influence of the three nations, Germany, Italy and Japan, on a map of the Eastern Hemisphere, it is possible to get a very clear idea not only of what has been going on in the world since the fall of France in May 1940, but also of how radically the military policies of the democracies must be changed if we are to defeat Hitler within the lifetime of this generation of Americans. For if we do this and if we have the courage to abandon our naval experts and look the facts in the face, we shall see how rash the democracies have been in occupying positions on the periphery of the area thus described. For with a minimum of risk, and depending on sea power to translate a basically false idea into colonies, bases, mandates, the British, French and Americans set up shop and started business in Manila, India, Saigon, Singapore, Hong Kong, all of which were on the periphery of what was to become, through the careful planning of Hitler, the sphere of influence of Japan, a nation of the Axis group with continental land power in Asia.

Because her policy was orientated by the myth of sea power England would establish outposts in Asia and for the same reason America would acquire the Philippines. But these outposts not only had no continental land power behind them, but they also constituted invasions of the sphere of influence of whatever nation happened to acquire continental supremacy in Asia. That nation might have been China or Russia. It turned out to be Japan, and when it happened, the outposts of empire became besieged fortresses which sooner or later, unless their parent nations gained continental supremacy, would have to capitulate. There were, of course, other alternatives. Britain and/or America could have launched a real continental attack on Japan before she achieved continental supremacy over China and while she was still vulnerable to attack from Russia. This question was put squarely before both nations by Mr. Stimson when he was Secretary of State in 1931, but nothing came of it.

The result (it is a very serious result indeed) is that Japan now holds a strong position on the continent of Asia. We sat by, furnishing her with oil and scrap iron while she disposed of China so that her continental supremacy was no longer threatened in that direction. And when the German attack on Russia neutralized the only other danger to that supremacy, Japan was ready to take on the United States and England at the behest of Hitler, whose position in Europe was such that he was badly in need of the only coin that Japan could offer in payment for services rendered.

The same situation held at the beginning of the war in 1939 for France, whose Asian empire also fell within the orbit of the Asiatic nation that was reaching out. It is now evident that Japan, with the assistance of Haushofer and the geopoliticians, had read history correctly up to a certain point. Japan knew that it was Rome's continental power, not her sea power, that gave her the victory over Carthage and she knew also that it was the failure of the Mohammedan land armies before Vienna, not the destruction of the Mohammedan fleet at Lepanto, that set the Crescent beneath the Cross in the sixteenth century. But with all of her land power on the continent that she aspired to dominate, and with all of the democracies' weaknesses in this respect on that same continent, Japan could do nothing without the assistance of Germany.

China she could take care of, and the wide-eyed lumbering democracies not only permitted her to do so but even assisted her. However, Russia's continental land power still hung like a sword suspended over her head and her final decisive action against the insolent "imperial" outposts which the democracies had set up, right at her front yard, depended on the neutralization of Russia by Hitler.

And here, let me point out, was a situation pregnant with tremendous potential tragedy, and absolutely without precedent in recorded history. What we had in effect was this: decisive military action in Asia by a nation (wholly outside the European comity) against the nations who for fifteen hundred years had been the pillars of Western Civilization was dependent upon the military action of two other nations of Europe, both of whom were members of the European comity. The Japanese attack on the democracies in Asia was a contingency of the German attack on Russia in Europe. This was a brand-new historical situation and, as the sequel demonstrated, it went right on being new. The world spirit, or *Weltgeist*, of Hegel must have gasped with amazement as he watched the amazing panorama unfold. Ghosts of Napoleon, Julius Caesar, Chinese Gordon, may well have murmured "No one ever saw anything like *this* before."

The Western democracies, trusting in their sea supremacy, had established outposts, bases, colonies far beyond the protective sphere of their continental land power. And when the nation whose continental sphere they had invaded was finally able to unleash a real military threat against them, they could do nothing else but defend, which, by hypothesis, was fatal, not necessarily to the nations themselves, England, France and America, but to their outposts, to the garrisons of these outposts, to the nationals living therein or near by and to the flow of supplies and strategic materials derived therefrom. There was one alternative in the strange and unparalleled situation that confronted the democracies in 1939. This Asiatic power which threatened their colonies, and later on would attack them, was dependent on a European power. Japan could do nothing in Asia (just as Italy was helpless in Africa) unless the continental armed might of Germany was supreme in Europe. Japan might threaten, she might as a last act of desperation attack the democracies in Asia (as Italy had already done in Africa) but, due to the unique and peculiar totalitarian lineup, such an attack could not possibly succeed if the continental land power of the democracies could be hardened into an offensive spearhead and plunged into the flank of Germany.

There were almost unlimited opportunities for doing this but none were taken. Right straight through, heedless of the storm warnings that were going on, at every point of the compass, the democracies elected to leave themselves wide open. They never concentrated for attack; all over the world they elected to defend. They would defend everything at once, Bangkok and Paris, Burma and Oslo,

Hong Kong and Bucharest, Singapore and London, Manila and Rio de Janeiro. In short, the democracies, trusting in sea power, would defend on the *periphery and at the center* at the same time, they would defend everywhere. The Axis would attack everywhere. And here again was something so stupendously stupid that once more history, which has recorded some strange things, has no parallel for the enormous dispersion of effort entailed by this "total" defense.

Ancient Greece had colonies within the sphere of influence of Persia and the Persians mobilized their continental land power against these colonies, besieged all of them and took some of them (notably Miletus) but the Greeks knew perfectly well what they were doing and took the necessary action at Platea and Marathon, and if they had not done so, we would all be wearing spade beards and offering sacrifices to Zoroaster right this minute. The Romans also had certain colonies in the Euxine (Black Sea) region, and these colonies were within the sphere of continental influence of a totalitarian dictator named Mithridates who resembled Adolf Hitler in more ways than it would be proper to enumerate outside of a medical treatise. Mithridates launched everything he had, and he had plenty, in an attack against Rome's outpost that for treachery, suddenness and sheer savagery makes Japan's attack on Pearl Harbor look like a game of Post Office. But the Romans also knew what they were doing, and they bored right into the center, aiming offensive land action at Mithridates' capital until it was clear to all concerned that a declaration of war which bore the superscripture SPQR meant exactly what it said.

Even more to the point than these "total wars" of the ancient world was the conflict fought in the seventeenth and eighteenth centuries between the absolutism of the Bourbons (*L'état c'est moi*) and the British notion of constitutional freedom. This conflict was waged in North America and India as well as in Europe, but it was not decided in North America or in India. Battles were fought on the periphery of Britain's sphere of influence (Louisburg, Quebec, Plassey), redskins were shot on the banks of the St. Lawrence and redcoats were slain at the mouth of the Ganges but it was the offensive continental land power of Britain launched at France *in Europe* which removed the "threat

of the Bourbon" forever. It was the attack of the
British expeditionary force under Marlborough
which so weakened French land power on the
continent of Europe that the French colonies of
North America, and the same thing goes for India,
fell quite naturally, as "accessories" always will,
into the lap of England.

Now it should not be difficult to draw the correct inference here. The British colonial expansion
of the seventeenth and eighteenth centuries was
made possible, the outposts which Britain established within the sphere of influence of France and
Spain were given permanence, the British civilization and the British common law were given a
firm foothold in the New World, not by British
sea power attacking on the perimeter of the imperial domain but by British continental land
power attacking at the center. In short, the fate
of Europe decided the fate of the outlying imperial possessions, and not vice versa. It was that
way then and it would be that way now if the
British had elected to attack Hitler say in 1936
(when he broke the Treaty of Locarno) as ag-
gressively as their ancestors attacked Louis XIV in
1702 (when he broke the Treaty of Partition).

The Reversal of History

No attack has been launched at the center and as a result we see, as I have pointed out, a situation without parallel in history. The fate of civilized Europe, the future of freedom-loving men, the heritage of two thousand years of political evolution, is now threatened by a conflict that is taking place in Malaysia ten thousand miles from the country where that conflict should be taking place. Because no decisive battles had been fought on the continent of Europe in the second quarter of the twentieth century a decisive battle had to be fought on an island in the Western Pacific.

Not since the barbarian chieftain Hermann defeated the Roman legions in the foothills of Westphalia has such a strange thing occurred. Never since the fifth century has the fate of so many people been placed in the balance by the stupidity of so few. It was thought by the pseudo-imperialists that as long as the ramparts of ocean could be held (what they really meant was that as long as the 5–5–3 naval ratio could be maintained) the outposts of Manila, Singapore, Hong Kong, were safe; the periphery of democracy was as safe as the center — which was just ducky until these ridiculous proconsuls stuck their scissor bills into the lair of an old curly-wolf of a real imperialist whose name was Adolf Hitler. When that happened the floating fortresses of steel turned out to be almost as useless as the fixed fortresses of concrete and it was discovered that sea power couldn't guard the provinces any better than defensive land power had protected the capitals.

The result was a complete reversal of historic military values. The tide of influential events, instead of running from the center to the periphery, or from the capitals (London, Washington) to the provinces (Hong Kong, North Africa, Singapore, Manila), began to run in the opposite direction. A defeat at Baguio or Lingayan or Cavite would have a decisive effect on the councils of statesmen in the White House, and bad news from Malaysia or North Africa would spell disaster to British and French ministers in Downing Street. Whether Manila could hold out or not, whether Singapore resisted or fell, whether Weygand kept or relinquished command, whether Dakar was taken by the Germans or by the Free French, whether Eritrea could be bombed or not — all of these things began to assume a prominence in world affairs comparable to that once held by the military operations of Julius Caesar or of Marshal Foch. Instead of showing some interest in what was going on in the center of Europe, men spoke with bated breaths of a retreat that was taking place in a tropical swamp or an advance made under cover of a desert sandstorm.

The center was controlled by the periphery, the tail was wagging the dog and due to a wholly false strategic idea and its persistence in the minds of men long beyond the time when it should have been abandoned, it was logical that this should happen. Is it not axiomatic that a false proposition carried to its logical conclusion will inevitably lead to an absurdity? In this case the conduct of the war against Hitler in Europe had been made to depend on defense; the adequacy of the defense had been made to depend on the shipment of war materials and supplies from America to the defending democracies, notably and principally England; but the shipment of finished war materials to England, the adequate arming of China, depended on the flow of strategic raw materials from the Far East which depended on the supremacy of British and American sea power in the Far East, which depended on the ability of this sea power to hold

Manila, Hong Kong, and Singapore without offensive continental land power, which was, as events have now shown, a manifest impossibility.

"*Voilà ce qu'arrive,*" said Napoleon, "*quand on entasse les défauts sur les défauts.*" If the democracies of the West had established continental land power in Asia ten years ago, Japan's hands would have been tied; if these democracies had advanced resolutely against Germany five years ago, the Axis would never have been formed; if the democracies had launched a decisive attack on Germany two years ago, everything would be over right now — except, of course, for the bickering of the diplomats over the peace table; if the democracies had even launched a decisive attack on Germany through the Balkans one year ago we would be well on the way to victory at the present moment. Indeed, this whole business of what the democracies should have done and did not do, this whole matter of what protective measures should have been taken, and were not taken, to insure the democratic way of life, is a good deal like the old story of the Books of the Cumaean sibyl whose price went up as their tale decreased until three times the original sum demanded for the complete set of nine was asked — and gratefully paid — for the last three.

Nations as well as individuals must pay for their mistakes and by all accounts we are certainly not going to escape scot free for the invitational weaknesses and criminal negligence of the past ten years. But now that we see the danger we should try, and try desperately, to avoid having to pay more heavily than is necessary. Above all should we make haste lest, in the end, the bill rendered by the Fates be more than we can pay, as we have already seen happen to a number of other nations since this war started. We must remember that navies are powerful and decisive in large dynastic national wars (England and Spain, sixteenth century) as well as in small pseudo-imperialistic wars (Japan and Russia, nineteenth century) but that in a really imperialistic total world war, such as we are now fighting, they are not, by any possible stretch of the imagination, decisive, and are only powerful when they are used, with proper air support, for the convoy and supply of armies. In short, they must be used skillfully, not for the dispersion of the armed force but for its concentration in a decisive continental theater.

CHAPTER IX

THE RESTORATION OF STRATEGY

I THINK it was Blücher who said that "In war sweat saves blood" — a maxim of the old muscle-driven tactics which some think outmoded by the blitzkrieg of today. It is possible, however, to coin an equivalent, if not a paraphrase, and for the warfare of the machine age, we can say "Surprise shortens war." We have not declared war on the Axis in order to indulge ourselves, for the next ten years, in a sort of universal and worldwide game of blood-letting, but rather that our colossal strength may be so used that it will quickly and mercifully tip the balance towards the victory and the peace of justice. Therefore, it is inconceivable that, swayed solely by our emotions and our desires (natural enough under the circumstances) to punish Japan, we should fail to throw our strength immediately, daringly and decisively, in the direction where it will do the most good, i.e. where it will be most likely to bring victory.

The Restoration of Strategy

There is no doubt, then, that we must strike towards Europe, that we must strike soon and hard, and there is no doubt either, or should be none, as to where the first blow should fall. For every signpost of victory points towards Italy as the objective of the coming American offensive. The Italian peninsula, as anyone can see by a glance at the map, lies in the strategic center of that world island which Hitler aspires to dominate. Without Italy, every hope of Nazi victory in Africa goes glimmering. Without Italy, German influence over Spain and Vichy-France is weakened, the Balkan conquests rendered insecure, the chains loosened on the limbs of Greece. And with Italy in the hands of the enemy, Turkey will surely come unstuck and join the Allies, and the Dardanelles, back door to Berlin, will be thrown wide open. Italy is the solar-plexus of the Axis, as Germany is its spearhead, and Japan its nether-end, and a right recognition of the tremendous strategic opportunity involved requires that we undertake immediately, without a glance at Dakar or Martinique or North Africa, the stupendous, breath-taking, history-making task of the invasion of Italy.

It is not without significance to us in our life-

and-death struggle with the New Caesarism that Rome ruled the world for five hundred years from the peninsula of Italy. And there is no doubt that Hitler, from the very beginning, has been thoroughly aware of the importance of this peninsula and the inland seas which it dominates. There is also ample evidence that he now realizes too late the danger to which his already tottering empire is exposed through this, its weakest member. Over-extended in Europe, his fighting forces attenuated by the necessities of guard duty in captive states, pegged down by the Russian campaign, he is now attempting to strengthen his bulwarks in the Mediterranean and is turning wistful eyes towards Spain and Portugal, but he can do nothing provided that America can be induced now, at the eleventh hour, to strike at Italy with all her force.

For observe, if Italy falls to us, the Mediterranean becomes, in very truth, *mare nostrum*, and the combined fleets of Britain and America can sweep every German raider (surface ship or submarine) from these seas; if Italy falls to us, Africa is safe, Suez is safe, the fear of a German occupation of Dakar and excursions against South America is removed "for the duration." If Italy falls to us, the boot is on the other foot with regard to the use of land-based aviation in all operations in Europe south of the sixtieth parallel. Take a map and see what this means: Quite literally it means that Hitler is caught between the upper and the nether millstones of British- and Italian-based American air power and can be ground into powder at our convenience. Most important of all, if Italy falls to us, we gain a real continental base for the major operations of land warfare in connection with (not isolated from) the operation of the Allied fleets. This is the real meaning of the relationship of sea power to empire — not the brittle pseudo empire of the Mahan theory, but the solid substantial *imperium* — the only sort of empire worth having — of Rome. To do this is to combine against Hitler the sea power of Nelson and the offensive land power of Napoleon.

This is the way that sea power should be used and in this particular case — the reduction of the Mediterranean stronghold of the Axis — we have a golden opportunity ready to our hand. There is no question but that England has long realized the presence of this opportunity on her very doorstep so to speak — but she was unable to take advantage of it for four reasons: (a) She could not deplete the defenses of England to gain the necessary man

power. (b) With Singapore and her Pacific possessions to guard, she could not bring into action the
necessary sea power. (c) She had already been
lured into a limited offensive in the Mediterranean
area (Greece) and had her fingers well and properly
burned. (d) She was already committed to a major
offensive in Africa deemed necessary for the protection of Suez and undertaken by that group of
strategists who still believe that Hitler can be defeated by striking at subsidiary objectives. It was
thought that Suez could be defended in Africa just
as it was thought that Greece and Yugoslavia could
be defended from Malta and Crete. Alas! It should
now be evident to anybody with the simplest
knowledge of strategy that the way to defend
Suez, as well as Dakar, is by mastery of the Mediterranean, and this cannot be achieved without the
possession of Italy.

2

It would take 200,000 men to start with, and
another 200,000 to follow every month until victory is achieved. It would take three fourths of the

American fleet, at least half of the British fleet, every bombing plane and every transport of both nations. It would take a plan for battle training that would put one field army every month in fighting trim, it would require initiative, resourcefulness, the ruthless cutting of red tape and above all — courage. But it could be done and not a thing in the world could be done to prevent it by Hitler or anyone else — provided it was done *in time*.

What I am saying is that if certain conditions are satisfied, we could have our victory program printed in large type and distributed to all the heads of state, with Hitler, Mussolini and Hirohito first on our mailing list; we could have the notice of the coming American Atlantic offensive broadcast by radio to all nations, with especial attention to the language difficulties of German, Italian and Japanese listeners-in; we could serve notice on all rogue-dictators and inform every single one of the male-factor peoples what we had in mind to do, how we intended to do it, when we intended to do it, and no military or naval effectives which they could muster, no counter measure which it is within their grasp to take, could slow us up by one second or narrow the scope of our effort by one inch. For

Hitler has finally miscalculated, the German Army has overextended itself, and the only hope for the Axis is in the chance that America, having persistently and stubbornly followed the wrong road for the last twenty years, will be unable to recognize the right road until it is too late to take it.

So if we turn away from Japan, and towards Europe, with our armed might, Hitler is already defeated. If we move in time, he will be as pegged-out, as staked-down, as helpless to prevent an American offensive in Italy as England was to prevent the German attack in the Balkans. In fact, Hitler is in exactly the same position now with regard to an American invasion of Europe as England was when the German Army advanced against Yugoslavia and Greece in the spring of 1941. Widely advertised as the war was — and quite literally the whole world was taken into Hitler's confidence — the British, fully committed in Africa to protect the Suez Canal, and anticipating a German invasion of England at any moment, could not possibly release sufficient effectives to make a Balkan victory certain or even probable. It was hoped that the Yugoslavs and the Greeks could hold, and there was even some hope that the mountainous nature of terrain over which the Germans must advance could offer a sufficient obstacle, but when those hopes proved vain, there was nothing Britain could do to save the situation which from a strictly military point of view (i.e. without reference to the broken stick of sea power) was lost from the very start.

The roles are now reversed. Hitler dare not relax his vigilance in Africa for a moment or he risks immediate loss of that continent to the English, who have now built up a formidable force there; he dare not release a single division from the Russian front lest his line, now being hammered for soft spots, suffer that fatal penetration which the Russians are so desperately seeking and to avoid which his armies have three times recoiled. His air power and such sea power as he possesses have now reached the point of extreme attenuation consonant with sound employment.

Everything points, therefore, to the spring of 1942 as the time the American blow should be delivered. The military effectives necessary for such a thrust, an armored motorized force of 200,-000 men, are immediately available for one month's battle training before the transports are assembled; the air force for their convoy and combat support is on hand. The follow-up force, the second 200,000, can be made ready within the time required (i.e. two months), and with American energy and resourcefulness we should have little difficulty in carrying out the balance of the victory program and satisfying the conditions imposed by this concept of strategy.

For one thing is certain: it will not be possible to unseat Hitler merely by defending, or by furnishing aid to his enemies (Britain in chief), or by nibbling at the border of his continental system. It was Hitler who evoked the revolutionary Napoleonic warfare from its tomb and made it win victories for him. It is the same sort of warfare that must now be used against him. Believing that America was irrevocably committed to isolationism, certain that he could control and direct such war effort as we were willing to make, certain that if the worst came to the worst, he could use his Japanese accomplice to abort our offensive effort into the Pacific, he has stretched his strategic lines over so much territory that the strands are beginning to part under the strain. This is the time to strike him before a victory over Russia (or over England) enables him to gather in his nets for another cast.

3

It should be clear now, indeed — if we had not been so bemused by the incantations of our isolationists and sea-power experts, it should have been clear long ago — that Italy's inclusion in the Axis was not due to Hitler's hope of gaining any considerable accretion of military strength from his alliance with Mussolini. On the contrary, and from a strictly military standpoint, Italy was actually a hazard. But it was a hazard that must be taken because of the geographical position of this country. The knife which the Italian assassin plunged into the back of France might just as well, in a different lineup, have been plunged into the back of Germany. Hitler knew this from the very first and it was the position of Italy — a position which made her the Achilles' heel of Germany — that has made Hitler so solicitous in cultivating the friendship of Mussolini, so careful not to offend Italian sensibilities, so prompt in dispatching aid to the assistance of this lame duck even when it was urgently needed elsewhere.

At any rate, this is the way to commence our battle with the Axis which has battened and grown insolent during the last two years on the failure of every limited offensive launched by the Allies. This is the thing to be done and not the least of the arguments in its favor is that it is something than can be done quickly provided we take it in hand with energy and resolution, and the truth is that every argument which might be urged against a Pacific offensive goes into reverse and points the other way when the question of an all-out American invasion of Italy comes up for consideration. Foremost among these considerations, as it must ever be in a thoroughgoing military treatment, are the important differences in the racial characteristics of the two nations Japan and Italy.

Now for many reasons it is all important for the initial American effort to be successful and I trust I shall not be accused of cowardice when I say that considered solely from the standpoint of the fighting qualities of the two nations, a major offensive against Italy is much more likely to be successful than an equally strong attack launched against Japan. In fact, such is the suicidal fanaticism of the Japanese that even if we are prepared to slay the entire nation, man, woman and child, a Japanese offensive is likely to give us considerable trouble at the present time no matter how much force we put behind it. For as Kipling pointed out long ago: if the enemy is determined to die, ardently desires to die in battle, and firmly believes that he will gain paradise by so doing, he has considerable edge on the soldier who, however brave, still has some sneaking fondness for life.

It is not that any of these suicide-minded juramentados, howling dervishes, followers of the Old Man of the Mountain, or committers of hara-kiri, have ever won out in the long run against the rational warfare of the Western tradition, but at the same time, in making our estimate of the situation, the fanatical devotion of the Japanese to their emperor is something that should not be neglected. It is part of rational warfare to consider how the objective may be gained by the least expenditure of human life. All of which is simply another way of saying that we should strike our first blow at Italy — Italy, whose people are heartily sick of war and who long for an opportunity to abjure both Hitler and Mussolini.

"The Italians," said Napoleon, whose extraordinary keenness of judgment extended to nations as well as to men, "The Italians are a *pantaloon* people." This short and concise statement gives us the key to the outstanding national trait which made the absurd career of Mussolini possible, as well as to the national weakness from which every Italian averts his eyes even in secret. For "pantaloon" as Napoleon used the word means "clown."

The Italians are clowns, that is to say buffoons, mimes, imitators, and it is this quality — it is, in a manner of speaking, a histrionic quality — that is responsible for the mushroom growth of Fascism and the rapidity with which Mussolini rose to power. The Italians responded readily to this "Duce" with his heady, intoxicating oratory about "a place in the sun" and the restoration of the "grandeur that was Rome." It was fine while it lasted, to march and wear red pants and shout; fine, too, to charge the horsemen of Haile Selassie with tanks and spray the Ethiopian goat-herds with mustard gas (a pretty bit of German imitativeness this!). But not so good later on at Guadalajara and still worse in the mountain passes of Greece. No! The Italians didn't like it when they encountered the real thing. One was reminded too forcibly of Caporetto. "Pantaleone" became sad. . . . Now it is this "sad clown" among the nations that occupies the most strategically important country on earth, a country that is ours, if not for the asking, then certainly for the taking.

These psychological considerations having to do with the Italian people themselves should influence our choice of the initial American theater of operations. There are others almost equally important which concern the state of mind and, more particularly, the morale of other peoples dwelling in the supremely important strategic area concerned, that is to say, along the Mediterranean and Adriatic littorals.

Are we to suppose, for example, that an American triumph over the imitation Caesar who is more cordially detested in Europe than Hitler himself will not waken the bludgeoned love of liberty in the breasts of Frenchmen, Greeks, Southern Slavs? Do you suppose that Spaniards who see their hard-won peace threatened by Hitler's and Mussolini's constant encroachments will not rejoice at the appearance of the American flag in the Mediterranean arena, with an American Army behind it? By all indications, it has not been with unmixed delight that Francisco Franco has watched the spread of Axis influence in the Mediterranean. With his country still in the convalescent stage from a bloody civil war, there was little he could do to prevent it. However, let us not forget that last April, when Señor Suner took it upon himself to arrange with Göring a plan by which Nazi flyers were to use Spain as an air base for their North African operations, it was the *Caudillo* himself who vetoed the agreement. "It was not," as Franco said, "in accordance with the honor of Spain," And this alone, if we had nothing else to go on, would give us an indication that if America launched a strong offensive in the Mediterranean it would not be altogether repugnant to the Spaniards.

The truth is that if we are to reawaken the sleeping spirit of revolt in the nations that lie within the orbit of the Axis, and this goes for certain wavering South American countries as well as for Spain and Vichy-France, we must encourage some more positive action in Europe than the secret scratching of "V's" on the sidewalks or the assassination of Nazi agents by intrepid *commandos*. It is time for some nation to say "Full steam ahead and damn the torpedoes." Until this is done, we cannot expect the "reduced democracies" of the European comity to make much headway with the "Victory" drive. There are many things that Spain can do, that the Free French can do, that the Yugoslavs and Greeks can do to give us material assistance and it would not be too much to expect a general uprising of the Nazi slave states coincident with the first major military victory won by our armies. But before this step is taken by the subject democracies of the continent, the free democracy of the Western Hemisphere must initiate some positive action.

As I have pointed out, these are all psychological considerations, reasons connected with the *morale* of the peoples whose ultimate fate, whether they like it or not, and whether we like it or not, is closely entwined with our own in the Great Game now being played in the uttermost corners of the earth. There are other reasons that apply with even greater cogency to the necessity of an American offensive being launched against Italy in the immediate future. These reasons are more strictly military and have to do with the application of force within certain sharp and defined limits of space and time. Chief among them is the great strategic principle of the concentration of effort.

4

It is impossible for an army, a nation, a fleet or a congeries of any one of these to be strong everywhere at once, which is precisely what England in her undue dependence on sea power has been trying to do for the past ten years. We also shall be guilty of this mistake if we throw too much strength in the Pacific, if we continue to look at North Africa as our major theater of operations, if we go on casting wistful eyes at Martinique or Dakar, *before we launch a major offensive at an active Axis member*. All of these things will come into our nets but they can only come after we have initiated some more decisive action, or taken a more positive risk. As long as the Axis holds its central positions undisturbed, the division of effort, the separation of forces involved, will deny to us the possession of any really important objective.

The nineteenth has been called "The Century of the Economists" just as our present epoch has been hailed as the end-term of that peculiar individual "economic man" for whom the laws of supply and demand represented ultimate values on this planet. One wonders, however, whether ideas which governed businessmen for so long in the conduct of their financial affairs did not exercise some influence over the sea strategy of a period absolutely unique in history. It is not without significance that some years ago General J. C. F. Fuller, Chief General Staff Officer of the British Tank Corps, published a treatise calling upon big business to guarantee world peace to the troubled nations through the exercise of "enlightened self-interest" among international financiers.

At any rate, it looks very much as though, in the conduct of operations up to the fall of Singapore, somebody had gotten hold of an economic idea and tried to make of it a military idea. Economically speaking, it is possible to be strong everywhere at once; economically speaking, the more agencies, the more subsidiaries, the more branches the parent business concern has, the less likely it is to fail in business, and *provided the international credit system holds,* a financier in London or New York can pick up his telephone and, in half an hour, effect a transfer of funds on the other side of the world which will put new economic life into a moribund agency.

Now when this concept of the international financiers (they also were pseudo-imperialists) was translated into strategy, the battle fleet of a great naval power would simply be assigned the same function as regards the protection of the threatened outposts of empire that the international credit system held in the economic fabric. If Singapore needed strengthening, Downing Street would issue an order by radio for two British battleships, H.M.S. *Prince of Wales* and H.M.S. *Repulse,* to repair immediately to Malayan waters. When that was done, everything would be all right, for who was better qualified to restore the threatened strategic balance than a British admiral? It all seems tragic nonsense now, in the light of what is happening in the Far East, but one wonders whether this business of applying economic concepts to strategy has been altogether done away with even in the

United States. Isn't it true that a good many of us still cling to the idea that it is a fine thing for the United States to furnish aid (it used to be "all-out aid short of war") for the threatened democracies all over the world? Isn't it true that many of us still think the war can be won that way?

But it can be shown, and conclusively shown, that this is simply another economic notion which is bound to vitiate and destroy all ideas of right strategy as long as it continues to be given a major role in this war. If the tried-and-true principles of strategy mean anything at all, this scattering of American supplies and American troops all over the periphery of Hitler's World Island, which is exactly what we are doing, means dispersion of effort. If we have not taken leave of every precept laid down by every successful captain, what is needed now is not dispersion of effort but concentration of effort. If military history from the Seven Against Thebes to the Second Battle of the Marne has any meaning, the best way to help China, the best way to defeat Japan, the best way to support Russia is to strike with the concentrated might of England and America at the chink in the Axis armor which is Italy.

Defense Will Not Win the War

A thousand objections will be raised to this method of waging war that is in direct contradiction to the preconceptions of the sea-power experts. To answer these and any other questions that may be raised, it will be sufficient merely to lift our eyes and look the facts in the face. It is upon the attenuation of the fighting strength of his enemies that Hitler has won his most important victories. At the present time, presuming upon the continuation of the British strategy of disaster and having miscalculated the time and space factors of the Russian campaign, Hitler has permitted his own forces to suffer this same overextension, and, seeing his error too late, has inspired the Japanese attack in the hope of deflecting attention from his weakness. Up to this time he has succeeded beyond all expectations in dispersing the British effort whenever he found it necessary to do so. He has always waved the red scarf in two places at once: Transcaucasia and Libya; Singapore and Suez; Yugoslavia and Egypt — he would rattle the saber of invasion and attack France, rattle it again and attack Russia — and every time he has done this the British bull has cheerfully obliged by charging in both directions.

The only question now is whether America, with

her tremendous resources of decisive man power, is going to let herself be snared in this game of cat's-cradle. Now I spoke above of looking the facts in the face. What exactly are the facts that should govern our strategy at the present moment?

First: The war is entering a phase where absolute offensive action, as opposed to limited offensive action, is bound to be decisive against the Axis.

Second: The possibility of absolute offensive action against the Axis is dependent upon the achievement of sea-air supremacy by the democracies.

Third: Sea-air supremacy, when achieved, is worthless unless it can be used to gain continental land power for the democracies.

Fourth: Continental land power, to be decisive, must be used in a theater where it can be employed offensively for the absolute defeat of the Axis.

The following corollaries may be drawn from these conclusions: —

First: America is not, for the time being, in danger of invasion by any power on earth and is therefore free to concentrate her strength in absolute offensive action against the Axis provided we have the means to do so.

Second: These means are at hand, for: —

(a) America is absolutely strong in man power;

(b) America is absolutely strong in sea power plus air power, provided that our sea-air power is used in conjunction with Britain.

Third: The absolute supremacy of American man power can only be achieved by concentrating American man power plus American sea-air power at the same point where Britain's sea-air strength is now concentrated — that is to say, in Europe.

Fourth: There is only one point in Europe where the sea-air strength of the two democracies may be used immediately to give the man power of America a real continental base for offensive operations against the Axis, that is to say, Italy.

It should be evident from the above that only by concentration in the sole theater where concentration is possible can we gain the fighting strength, all elements considered, to launch a real offensive. Of course, it is impossible to foresee, and to prepare in detail, for all the contingencies that we shall encounter in the conduct of the continental war that will follow, but we may be sure of two things: given a real objective, American resourcefulness and initiative can be counted upon to overcome unforeseen difficulties as they arise — which is nine tenths of the art of war (according to Napoleon). And finally, we can be sure that every carefully prepared plan of the enemy will have to be scrapped in the face of offensive action by America which has been, there is no doubt about this, left completely out of account both by the geopoliticians who prepare Hitler's plans of conquest and the strategists who execute them. In this connection, we may well remember in the hour of crisis which is now upon us the unparalleled success of the French salient at the Second Battle of the Marne, where the most carefully prepared plans of Ludendorff were wrecked by a simple decision to attack. And so, taking reverently the torch of classic strategy from the hands of the last of the great captains, we may say with Foch: —

"In memoriam, in spem."

ON THE DANGERS OF WARFARE BY COMMITTEE

WE FIGHT again, this time not only in the battle of Europe but of the world. And since the method and manner of American intervention in the great conflict with the Axis is of supreme importance, it should be of interest to review briefly certain events of the First World War. They are not, it must be admitted, particularly pleasant events to recall but it is possible that thoughtful consideration of them may be highly salutary. If, for example, we could answer the question *What was happening in England and France during the years 1914–1917 which rendered the defeat of the Entente certain without the military and economic assistance of America?* we might be in a better position to solve the problem upon which our hopes of victory are hung in the present war: How are we to unleash our military might and support our allies to the limit while avoiding the dangers of divided counsel and frustration of effort which, in the past, have always attended the warfare of coalitions?

Clausewitz had said that "war is the continuation of *policy* by other means" but even Clausewitz in his wildest dreams of *Weltmacht* never imagined that war might be the continuation of *politics* by other means. It had never entered the head of the author of *Vom Krieg* that generals might be used as stalking horses by statesmen, that armies might be sacrificed like pawns to bolster the prestige of a propertied class, that a ruinous campaign such as that of Gallipoli might be undertaken, that a tragic blood-letting like the Nivelle offensive might be countenanced to maintain a party in power or to uphold a tottering ministry. The warfare by committee, the influence of political fears, hatreds and prejudices on the making and breaking of generals and marshals, wholly irrespective of their worth (or the lack of it) in the field, the formulation of military plans in accordance with political ambitions — such were the sinister and malign influences which operated to raise the Allied casualty lists to astronomical proportions without a single decision on the western front, such were the causes destined to result in the inevitable defeat of the Allied Armies had America not intervened in the eleventh hour.

The concept of war held by Clemenceau and Lloyd George was the exact counterpart of the sort of power wielded by the governments of France and of England. And just as the former was a throwback to the old dynastic warfare of the seventeenth and eighteenth centuries (and indeed by its very nature it could be nothing else) so the latter was pieced out and held together by the same makeshifts that ministers had used two hundred years before. There was only one difference: where a Colbert, a Richelieu or a Buckingham sought to maintain his personal power by flattering or otherwise placating a reigning monarch, the war ministers of England and France had to support their prestige by placating a ruling class. The old dynastic feudalism overthrown by the revolutions of 1691 and 1793 had returned under a new form.

Time out of mind decisive battles had been lost, blood had been spilled, and countries devastated in the name of a fiction called "dynastic interest" or "legitimacy." This time it was called *liberalism*. Where formerly a monarch had held sway and squandered blood and treasure by virtue of the blood-royal, a class now sought to control the destinies of nations, conscript armies and wage war by virtue of its wealth and material interests. And those precepts which had been invented by skillful legalists to permit the dynasts an arbitrary freedom of action that set them above the law and amounted to anarchy were simply exchanged for a more up-to-date group of shibboleths such as "Imperial Interest" and the "Defense of the Realm" that excused the most glaring faults of ministries and conferred a comfortable anonymity on high-placed dunces.

It was in this manner that what was nothing more than class rule at its worst, with all the attendant vices of oligarchy, was converted into the fiction of a national government. How was it possible that the conflict of counsel which prevailed behind this false front of liberalism should not have manifested itself in the conduct of the war? It is true that all these criminal mistakes, errors of judgments, flights of fancy of the glittering politicians that had to be paid for in human blood, were very successfully concealed at the time. Certainly America entered the war in complete ignorance of

all the mare's-nest of futility and folly that had
been dignified for three years as the "war policies"
of the European democracies. But we know all
about it now.

All the now-it-can-be-told books have been published, we have the recriminations of Lloyd George
and Earl Haig and the animadversions of Clemenceau and Poincaré. We know why Joffre was
limogé, and why Marshal Lyautey had to be
brought all the way from Morocco to hold for
three days the Baton which Nivelle relinquished;
we know what was behind the mutiny of the
French Army before Verdun and what Colonel
Repington thought of the "glittering politicians"
and we know that the war had not been in progress
for three months before practically every member
of the British and French ministries had his pet
general slated for supreme command, his pet plan
which would bring immediate victory and even his
pet weapon which was guaranteed to annihilate the
armies of the central powers while enriching the
munition-making friends of its sponsor.

As for the two Prime Ministers, Clemenceau and
Lloyd George, who were manfully endeavoring
to ride the whirlwind of the greatest war of history,

without sufficient principles between them to have equipped one well-intentioned gangster, *they* too had their mandates from the ruling classes of their respective countries to win the war and they too had their candidates for high command, their ideas of grand strategy, their fearful and wonderful notions of how Ludendorff was to be defeated, the Kaiser hanged and Germany squeezed "until her pips were heard to squeak," but above all and beyond all these relatively minor matters their patriotic souls burned with a holy fervor to remain in power.

Was Joffre a stupid general, who tactically speaking hardly knew his right hand from his left and whose woeful blunders at the First Marne would have inevitably lost that battle had it not been for the genius of Foch? Yes! but Papa Joffre, with his bovine serenity, his everlasting good humor, his Olympian calm, was the idol of the French Bourgeoisie — the controlling class in French politics, the anonymous but none-the-less real masters of Clemenceau. It was poor policy but good politics to leave him in command and he was left in command.

Was Foch the military genius who saved the

First Battle of the Marne, won the Bataille du Nord — being always twenty-four hours and one army corps ahead of the Germans — and warned Sir Henry Wilson against the Gallipoli Campaign? Yes, but Foch, in spite of his ability, was considered by the politicians to be a "dangerous" man, a man of metaphysical tendencies, who would not stand without being hitched — so it will be three years, years of defeat and huge casualties, before he will be called to the supreme command. Meanwhile the warfare by committee will continue.

There is no connected, orderly recital of the chain of events that led to the Allied victory. Because of his love for his country, Foch himself went to his grave without revealing, except in a few scattered utterances, faithfully taken down by Bugnet and Recouly, the depth of the abyss which time after time opened under his feet. Clemenceau, himself, perhaps unwittingly, gives the whole wretched story away in that final, vitriolic burst of spleen-letting, *The Grandeur and Misery of Victory*. And in many other personal reminiscences, memoirs and narratives of the war years, while there is no conscious effort to describe what was actually going on, there are a good many revelations, which any discriminating reader may discover for himself, of the way war should *not* be conducted. Following the example set by Clemenceau, Lloyd George, Joffre, Poincaré, Pétain were all so intent on self-vindication, so anxious for postwar political success, that they all unwittingly condemned themselves and their order to the execration of posterity.

2

I certainly do not intend to write, or even to outline, the military history of these eventful years at this time. I would, however, point out their tremendous importance for our present world, which is wading steadily deeper and deeper into war. And particularly would I indicate their significance for America at the present time. For they show, more clearly than was ever shown before, the difficulties and dangers which beset the warfare of a coalition.

In this warfare by committee, it was always my general against your general, my plan against your plan with little or no consideration for which general was the most demonstrably efficient, or which plan was objectively, i.e. as regards the hard realities of the situation, the *best* plan. Long before Foch was given the supreme command, he had demonstrated his strategical ability, his objectivity, his sense of the thing to be done, his cool, clear rationality, his unshakable will, his faith in God. Already, at the First Battle of the Marne, he had dispatched to the wavering Joffre his now famous message, "My right is exposed, my left is heavily attacked, my center is unable to hold its position. I cannot redistribute my forces. The situation is excellent. I shall attack." Already he had had his classic meeting with the feckless Sir John French at Ypres, answering the latter's complaint that he had no troops to withstand the German onslaught with the terse offer: "I bring you mine."

Now, the all-important question which springs inevitably to the military mind is this: why was Foch not given the supreme command at some time during the years 1914, 1915, 1916, 1917, or, failing this, why was not his constantly reiterated advice concerning the conduct of operations on the western front heeded by the statesmen who were trying to win the war from Downing Street and the Quai d'Orsay? Why was it that even after he was made generalissimo at the eleventh hour his plans were hampered and his counsels derided, his orders disobeyed and his recommendations disparaged by the very men, Clemenceau and Lloyd George, who were responsible for his selection as Commander-in-Chief? Why was it that he was given what was perhaps the heaviest responsibility ever placed on the shoulders of one man since the beginning of time without any real authority over the generals, Haig and Pétain, nominally under his command? Could not one of these politicians have found the courage to say of Foch what Lincoln had said of Hooker, "Let him win me some battles and I will hold his horse's bridle for him," or of Grant when the name of some political general was urged upon him, "Leave me this man — he fights"?

The parallel here is important for we shall find in it, not only the answers to the question posed above, but also the essential element of difference between the pseudoliberal or oligarchical and the truly democratic way in war. Foch, for example, was above all a soldier. His objective was the enemy's army; his mission the crushing of the enemy's will to war. What effect his strategy had on the course of French or British politics, whether Lord Beaverbrook praised in the *Daily Mail* or Horatio Bottomley blamed in *John Bull*, what *Le Rire* or *Le Matin* said about his conduct of the war mattered nothing whatsoever.

Take, for example, the much-discussed affair of the brigading of American regiments in French and British divisions and the attempt of Clemenceau and Lloyd George to prevent Pershing from having an army and a front of his own. It is possible to see in this incident alone the vicious effect of politics on the waging of war, and if this controversy over the parceling out of American troops were the only example of the division of counsel that prevailed among the Allies due to the erosion of politics, it would still be sufficient to condemn the pseudoliberal method of warfare. Why is this true?

It is true because war is absolute and the methods of waging it should only be determined with regard to a single object — the defeat of the enemy. Any considerations, political or otherwise, which are allowed to obscure the end or to weaken the means at hand will, in the long run, be self-defeating. That is to say they will result in an inevitable delay in attaining the objective, will prolong the conflict and show up tragically, at a later date, in terms of killed and wounded. In the case we are considering, Clemenceau wanted the newly arrived American regiments split up and assigned to French and British sectors. Foch resisted this idea and supported Pershing's demand for an autonomous American Army and a separate American front. The reasons which guided Clemenceau, and to a lesser degree Lloyd George, were *political* reasons; the reasons which stiffened Foch's resistance were purely *military* reasons.

The two premiers knew better than anyone else the war-weary temper of the French and English peoples. They knew what a master stroke of domestic policy it would be if it were officially announced that the depleted ranks of the French and English Armies were being filled by fresh American cadres and that everywhere along the front the decimated and shaken regiments of the Entente were being relieved and sent back to rest areas for rehabilitation. From the standpoint of the politician, it was a fine idea — an idea that could be cashed immediately in renewed public confidence in the "Government," that is to say, in a distinct increase of power for the two gentlemen who were most interested: Clemenceau and Lloyd George.

But this brilliant political idea was a very poor military idea and it was for this reason that Foch opposed it — opposed it so bitterly as to merit the epithet "Insubordinate" from the "Tiger," who for the first time, though not the last, found his will rebuffed and set at naught by a stronger personality than his own. Armies, reasoned Foch, fight better under their own generals and with their own objectives, and when he was directed by Clemenceau to cable President Wilson demanding Pershing's relief because "Black Jack" was unable to share Clemenceau's views on the disintegration of the American Army, he quite properly refused.

On the British side, we see the pseudoliberal method of conducting military operations in the constant bickering that went on between Lloyd George and Douglas Haig. Haig was a poor general, and it has now been revealed that the Prime Minister was well aware of this fact from the very start. However, he was not relieved, and the reason lies in the nature of the political power which the *soi-disant* British "Government" wielded during the war. This was, as I have pointed out, a sort of pseudo-sovereignty, wholly dependent for its authority on the very class which Haig represented.

After the war, it was all very well for Lloyd George, H. G. Wells, and Liddell Hart to rail at the stupidity of the "Cavalry generals" at the front. The point I am making is that at the time when Haig was sending divisions to certain death in the mud of Paschendaele and Loos, Lloyd George, who knew about it and held the highest position in the realm, could do nothing to prevent it because of political pressure. That is exactly what oligarchical or pseudoliberal warfare means and that is exactly why the First World War would have been disastrously lost for the Entente had it not been for the miracle of Foch and the American Army.

It was Foch who, disobeying and even defying Clemenceau, started the German hosts down the "inclined plane." It was Foch who refused to mutilate strategy by accepting the Procrustean prescriptions of brummagem politicians. We can still hear his strident voice ringing through the Hôtel de Ville at Doullens: "I would fight the Germans in front of Amiens; I would fight them in Amiens;

I would fight them behind Amiens." We can still take clean, unsullied delight in his classic reply to the emissary of Clemenceau who demanded to know his plans for future operations: "Tell M. Clemenceau that if he would know what I am going to do the day after tomorrow, he must come back tomorrow." We can see him again on the eve of the Second Marne with Mangin's strategic advance guard at the point of the salient "like a panther crouching on a limb."

Foch orders the French and British Armies forward, yet is not content merely to issue orders but proceeds in person to the Headquarters of Haig and Pétain, finding the former unwilling to advance, the latter actually ordering a withdrawal. We can see him exhorting and pleading where it should have been sufficient for him merely to have issued a laconic order from his Headquarters at Bonbon — and doing all this, accepting this tremendous responsibility in the full knowledge that he had no standing with the "Government" (Clemenceau was at that very moment meditating his replacement by Pétain) and that if his offensive failed, his official neck would be on the block within twenty-four hours.

3

There is, I insist, an important point here that must be grasped if we are to understand what happened at the Second Marne, July 18, 1918. And in this connection, I would stress the complete and wholehearted acceptance of responsibility by Foch in a situation where one false step meant, not only personal disgrace, but what was infinitely worse — military defeat and the loss of the war for the Allies, whose governments could not have outlasted the capture of Paris and the separation of the British and French Armies. That the war was ultimately won; that Ludendorff suffered defeat in the field, while the solidarity of the home front broke behind him owing to the effect of the American entry on the mind of the German citizen, was due to Foch's continued, unremitting wielding of the authority which he had, so to speak, usurped.

For, once Mangin's offensive turned out to be a success, Pétain hurled the remainder of the French into the fight and Haig could not, for very shame, withhold the British from taking their share in the only truly decisive action of the war. Pershing was already pushing forward in the Argonne, and with the Germans started down the "inclined plane" there was no power under Heaven strong enough to withstand the will of the man who was now generalissimo in fact as well as in name. The world, including the French and English politicians, could simply watch with stupefaction the dispositions of a strategist who in the space of four months had changed the futile, frustrate, ineffectual pseudo-liberal method of conducting military operations into authoritative leadership. It was the same strategist who dictated the terms of the armistice which, had they been rigidly enforced, would have put it forever beyond the power of Germany to threaten the civilization of the West. If the fruits of victory were afterwards lost, if Foch's strident voice demanding a Rhine frontier for France went unheeded in the babble of the peacemakers, if the gravest defeat which democracy has ever suffered took place around the council tables of Versailles, there is fortunately still time for America to learn the lesson and heed the warning that is written in these events.

I have called attention to the tragic results of the warfare of 1914–1917 as waged by the Allies in order to show the dangers attending the conduct of military operations by a nation, or by a coalition of nations, whose governments, whatever their outward form, are controlled by class-conscious oligarchies. For pseudoliberalism, or pseudodemocracy, is bound by its very nature to suffer the curse of divided sovereignty. What is called the "state" is merely a name to cover the clashing ambitions of the factions which constantly threaten the supremacy of the party in power. In the subterfuges, compromises and expedients which held men like Chamberlain and Daladier in office, the "people" have very little to say and the men who control events of tremendous importance, such as the British failure to apply the "oil sanctions" against Italy, or the French failure to attack when Germany began the remilitarization of the Rhineland, very often remain anonymous. No one has yet been able to give any reason for the removal of an efficient War Minister like Hore-Belisha, who had effected a miracle in revitalizing the moribund British Army, except that his personality was obnoxious to certain cabinet members. One wonders just what would have happened to the Union had Lincoln, in a similar situation, removed Grant from command because he was thoroughly disliked by so many of the "best people."

Hitler, Mussolini, *et al.*, following the lead of their mentor Oswald Spengler, are thus far right when they discant at great length on the fatal weakness of such political forms. The truth is that pseudodemocracy, precisely because it is lacking in authority, will move from defeat to defeat in time of war unless, as was the case in 1918, it is corrected by truly responsible, that is to say truly democratic, leadership. Moreover, if this is true, the corollary to it is also true and we can say with confidence that the ability of any *soi-disant* democratic government to harden into the spearhead of authoritative and responsible leadership is the unmistakable hallmark of its authenticity.

Before this Republic can fight, it must produce a leader, who, for the time being and as regards the conduct of operations, will be influenced by no considerations other than the defeat of the enemy. Accepting the fullest responsibility for his actions, he must also be capable of wielding, and, if necessary, seizing, absolute authority in all matters pertaining directly or indirectly to the conduct of the war, trusting always to the people (rather than to the politicians) for his mandate. Since the demands of strategy are absolute and the awful logic of battle brooks no compromise, there must be no *arrière-pensée* directed towards the field of domestic politics, no ear half-turned towards the oracles of the market place or forum. While General Mack listens to the confused mutterings of the Aulic Council, the Austrian Army at Ulm is being surrounded by Napoleon. Shall Hohenlohe advance on Lannes at Jena, or retreat towards Berlin? The King is of one opinion, the Queen holds another, while Brunswick vacillates and Blücher bites his nails in exasperation. In the end nothing is done until Napoleon arrives on the *Landgrafenberg* and settles matters in a characteristically military fashion. What use is it for Louis Napoleon (in 1870) to decide upon an advance of the French Army with the Empress Eugénie and the Council of State in Paris unwilling to take the risk and countermanding his orders? Result: the French genius for the offensive is cooled at Gravellotte — the most bloodily indecisive battle of history — Bazaine is shut up in Metz and capitulates; MacMahon is surrounded at Sedan without striking a blow.

Here we reach the typical, though by no means

hopeless, weakness of democracy. It is a weakness of nature which must be corrected by courage. It is a fault springing from a too easy way of life that must be corrected by stern disciplines that a free people should rejoice to impose on itself. The truth is that for a democracy, war is the touchstone, not only of the republic's ability to survive but also of its *right* to survive. This moment of awful choice which binds and looses history will unfailingly and inevitably demonstrate whether or not a nation is a real or merely a pseudodemocracy. That France was in the latter category, England, for all of her aristocratic trimmings, in the former, the march of events has now proved beyond peradventure of a doubt.

At present we are suffering from the handicap that every democracy is under when confronted with the exigencies of warfare made against a government of the Caesarist type. Where Caesarism enters the combat with all the resources of the state at the command of a single man, the democracy must first undergo an evolutionary, sometimes even a revolutionary, operation and perform an act which, because of its accompanying travail, might well be compared to the act of giving birth. Before the republic can fight with any hope of success it must unite behind a leader who for the time being and as regards the conduct of military operations will be influenced by no considerations other than the defeat of the enemy's field forces. We have had such leaders in the past, and we have one today in the person of Franklin D. Roosevelt. All that is necessary now is the will of the nation that should harden into the "thrice-hammered hardihood in arduous things" which his leadership deserves.

THE END